ASSEMBLING THE PIECES

SUPERCHARGING UNITARIAN UNIVERSALIST SOCIAL ACTION COMMITTEES

D0684426

GARY D. NISSENBAUM

First Edition, May 2011

© copyright 2011 G.D. Baum, LLC

ISBN-13: 9781460962183
ISBN-10: 1460962184
LCCN: 2011903380

All rights reserved. No portion of this work may be re-produced in any manner whatsoever without the ex-press permission of the author. No claim is made to any affiliation with, or representation of, any person or organization, such as without limitation, the Unitarian Universalist Service Committee, the Unitarian Univer-salist Association or the Unitarian Church in Summit.

To Roberta,
with love everlasting bathed in soft shades of emerald
green and the distant sound of Adagio for Strings.

In the fleeting time we have on this earth, what matters is not wealth, or status, or power, or fame – but rather, how well we have loved, and what small part we have played in bettering the lives of others.

President Barack Obama
2011

One of the sayings in our country is Ubuntu - the essence of being human. Ubuntu speaks particularly about the fact that you can't exist as a human being in isolation. It speaks about our interconnectedness. You can't be human all by yourself, and when you have this quality - Ubuntu - you are known for your generosity.

We think of ourselves far too frequently as just individuals, separated from one another, whereas you are connected and what you do affects the whole world. When you do well, it spreads out; it is for the whole of humanity.

Archbishop Desmond Tutu
2008

TABLE OF CONTENTS

William F. Schulz, President and CEO,
Unitarian Universalist Service Committee, March 2011

"By their groups shall ye know them!" That was a favorite expression of the great Unitarian Universalist social ethicist James Luther Adams (1901–1994). Riffing off the familiar phrase from the Gospel of Matthew, "by their fruits [sometimes rendered 'works'] shall ye know them," Adams was making the points that by ourselves we can accomplish relatively little and that the quality of a society can be measured in part by the nature of the groups — what Adams called "voluntary associations" — found within it. Societies that have an overabundance of cultural groups, like folklore circles or arts societies, and a dearth of political advocacy groups, for example, are likely to lack what today we would call the infrastructure of "civil society" sufficient to resist an oppressive government. Jim was a fierce champion of voluntary associations, particularly those devoted to social justice.

Gary Nissenbaum has written a book about one particular kind of group — social action committees within congregations — and suggests, at least by implication, that you can know something important about the congregation as a whole by measuring the quality of its social-action efforts. Moreover, he makes it clear that congregations — groups in themselves — can increase their effectiveness as advocates for social justice immeasurably when they find ways to connect with other groups outside their walls.

But Gary knows that you don't have to go far in this world to find a dysfunctional group. Social action committees have been among the most exemplary of that truism. So Gary has set out to help fix that. He says, quite rightly, that much of what he has to offer is common sense, but it is, unfortunately, common sense too often ignored. With a combination of practical insights, telling examples, and good humor, *Assembling the Pieces* aims to make it harder for anyone to claim they don't know how to make a social action committee work. (And, by the way, much of Gary's common sense applies to other committees as well.) You may not agree with everything Gary proposes, but you can't help but admire his levelheadedness.

I'm particularly grateful for his insistence that we ought not allow the enormity of the world's problems to discourage us from tackling a small part of them. I have often told the story of the horseman who came upon a tiny sparrow lying on the ground with her feet sticking straight up into the air. "Whatever are you doing?" asked the horseman. The sparrow explained that she had heard that the sky was falling and she was preparing to hold it up. "How ridiculous," scoffed the horseman. "Your two puny little legs holding up the whole sky?" "Well," said the sparrow chirpily, "one does what one can! One does what one can!"

The proof of the wisdom of what Gary offers of course is in the doing — and here the Unitarian Church in Summit, N.J. is worthy of a few hundred "hosannas." Some of those, I'm pleased to say, have been earned in collaboration with the Unitarian Universalist Service Committee, and we are enormously grateful for that. But, as Gary assures us, it is not his point (nor is it mine) to toot particular horns; it is rather to make the whole orchestra perform more melodiously.

If that happens, our groups will be more effective; the group experience more rewarding; justice better served; and James Luther Adams, God bless him, inordinately proud!

Foreword

Rev. Vanessa Rush Southern, Parish Minister
The Unitarian Church in Summit, March 2011

When we asked Gary to Chair our Social Action Committee I was sure he would say "no." He had a thriving law practice, his hands full fighting some of the leading civil liberties cases pro bono for New Jersey's branch of the ACLU, and a life of friends and family and fiction writing on the side. For me this experience will stand as proof of the advice to ask people anyway and let them decide. Gary put a couple of key conditions on his acceptance (another great lesson to me about how to equip our lay people for greatness) and took off.

I would have said our folks were too busy to do too much for the world. I would have said that it was the job of a few – of staff and a couple of lay leaders – to make a respectable number of opportunities possible for folks to serve the larger world. What I did not take into account is how powerless and existentially sad many folks feel when facing the brokenness and pain in the world. What I did not take into account was how much they wanted to believe, and live into the promise that we truly can still make a difference.

What Gary made room for was a caring, supportive, but action-oriented group that gave every lay leader with a dream the authority and responsibility for making it a credible possibility for us to live into that dream.

Upset about hunger? Tell us what we can do and where and we will marshal the congregation behind you.

Appalled by the crisis in education? What bite can we take out of the issue?

It might not look like much at first, but seeing a fellow member lead the charge to unravel problems bit by bit and bite by bite builds up the muscles of hope and determination in a people. Despair turns back into resolve. Surrender gets pushed aside by fierce love that rises from its slumber. And you walk a little taller. And in this case, a whole congregation walks taller.

We often talk about vicious cycles, but this would be one of those less touted forces in the universe, the virtuous cycle. She starts off slow and builds momentum and then you get to just sit back and watch the magic. Last month we set an ambitious goal of $8500 to build an orphanage in Haiti. When the dust settled over $11,000 had come in. We weathered our third transition in Principals in the school with which we partner every year, and two snow cancellations, and still had record numbers of tutors present to show the students that they and their learning matter to more than just them. And each month a new person comes to check out the Social Action Committee. If they are anything like the dozens who have come before, they'll offer an idea they have about some work we can do or about a problem we cannot stand by anymore without a collective response, and Gary will say, "Come back with a plan next month of what we can achieve and what you need to do so. Welcome aboard!"

And the wheel spins even faster.

Gary D. Nissenbaum, Chair, Social Action Committee
The Unitarian Church in Summit, March 2011

Recently, a number of lay leaders at the Unitarian
Church in Summit were asked to read a short statement
explaining why they are Unitarian Universalists. Here is
what I presented.

Why I am a Unitarian Universalist

*In thinking about why I am a Unitarian Universalist, I
am reminded of the words of my favorite author, Henry Miller.
In his novel, Sexus, he writes,*

> *Every man, when he gets quiet, when he becomes
> desperately honest with himself, is capable of ut-
> tering profound truths. We all derive from the
> same source. There is no mystery about the ori-
> gin of things. We are all part of creation, all
> kings, all poets, all musicians; we have only to
> open up, only to discover what is already there.*

*Too often, our experience of Western religion, rightly or
wrongly, is that it doesn't open us up; instead, it closes us down.
It creates rules and boundaries that are meant to prevent our
capacity to sin, that are meant to help us gain control of our
evil side. Too often, it fears the unbridled expression of what is
inside of us. It teaches that we need to discover the truths outside of us, those contained in a holy book, or the instruction of a
trained, religious leader or the writings of ancient patriarchs.*

*I am a Unitarian Universalist because none of that reso-
nates with me. I want to be in a congregation that is ready to
open itself up to the social action so desperately needed in the*

world around it; to open itself up to all nature of diversity both in who we are and what we believe; to open itself up to the discovery of what wondrous things are already there, within each of us.

As I see it, we are born alone, and we die alone. Bringing meaning to what happens in between, putting our lives to a proper purpose, so to speak, is our highest personal responsibility. In short, we must work out our individual destinies, and in doing so, as Miller also wrote, "nobody can be of any help except by being kind, generous, and patient."

I come to this congregation because I want to explore matters of spiritual growth with people who are kind, generous and patient.

What We Did in Summit

At the 2010 General Assembly of the Unitarian Universalist Association, our congregation received the Unitarian Universalist Service Committee's Social Action Award. It was the first year such an award was given. We were also one of only two large congregations to receive the Unitarian Universalist Association's Breakthrough Congregation Award.

The purpose of writing this book is not to take credit for that achievement. No one person deserves individual credit. As with most endeavors, great things happen when an energized set of peers work in concert for the common good.

Instead, I am writing this book to suggest ways that our success can be replicated in other congregations. What we did in Summit, New Jersey was only one of many ways to energize a Unitarian Universalist Social Action Committee. Many Unitarian Universalist congregations are larger and more accomplished in this area than we. Many do it better. Ours is only one way, offered for what help it can give.

You Are Holding an Example of Social Action

Marshall McLuhan wrote that "the medium is the message." The book you are holding is an example of one of its own messages: that we must accomplish social action in creative ways. I am self-publishing this text. That will allow us the freedom to donate copies at cost, without royalty, for Unitarian Universalist causes. Self-publishing allows us to use this book for directed fund-raising.

For example, if you purchase this book through the Unitarian Universalist Service Committee (UUSC), you are donating to a fundraiser being coordinated by a partnership of UUSC and our Social Action Committee. In this way, our mission of larger service multiplies.

We consider this to be another innovative way to work with UUSC. It is in keeping with our entrepreneurial approach to outreach. But it is only one of many potential initiatives. There are other creative ways to undertake social action that I hope you will discover on your own. I wrote this book to serve as a catalyst for that process.

The Structure of this Book

It is not necessary to read this book in a unitary fashion, no pun intended. Instead, I urge you to pick and choose which parts speak to your congregation's social action needs. Reverend Lewis B. Fisher said, "Universalists are often asked where they stand. The only true answer is that we do not stand at all ... We move around." I urge you to move around this book to find what is important to you.

In the first seven chapters (which loosely correspond to the seven principles of Unitarian Universalism), I will set forth specific aspects of growing a typical small to medium-sized Unitarian Universalist Social Action Committee into an effective instrument of change. For ease of reference, I have organized the chapters as offering solutions to discreet challenges generally facing such Social Action Committees. I conclude with a short discussion of my personal journey to becoming involved in this work.

These seven challenges will not nearly be an exhaustive list. However, as the saying goes, the perfect is the enemy of the good. I shall attempt to set out a direction toward the goal of supercharging a Unitarian Universalist Social Action Committee, one of many possible ways of getting there. Not the best and not the worst, but good enough. It worked for us.

I am the first to admit that much of what I have written will seem like common sense to most readers. Having said that, I think some of it will be new.

I am continually surprised when members of Social Action Committees of other congregations approach me and ask for my advice. Their Committee is barely making it. It is broken in one way or another. They do not know what to do to fix it. They know they are making mistakes, but they cannot define the exact nature of those mistakes, nor discern the precise way to address them.

These are challenges that can be solved. I want to present a simple and straightforward way to do so. In essence, the seven chapters that follow are meant to provide a simple tool box, as it were, for Social Action Committees that are off course and need an adjustment to get back on track.

I have been asked to maintain the anonymity of persons to whom I refer in this book. Many of them are members of the Social Action Committee who have done an extraordinary job of leading our initiatives. While I would prefer to refer to them by name, I am honoring their wishes to maintain anonymity. Nevertheless, what follows is not my story, but our story.

If one person takes one idea from this book and uses it to help one person who would otherwise have gone without, then this book has been a success.

1

THE FIRST CHALLENGE

How do we Integrate the Vision of the Social Action Committee Into the Consciousness of the Congregation?

We covenant to affirm and promote the inherent worth and dignity of every person.

Excerpt from the By-laws of the Unitarian Universalist Association

Affirming and Promoting the Inherent Worth and Dignity of Every Person.

Our Social Action Committees often pull away from trying to garner congregational buy-in. They may begin to move increasingly in their own direction without broad congregational involvement or awareness. When this happens, the results can cause the inevitable resentment on both sides.

On the other hand, putting all major decisions of the Committee to a congregational vote would not be a good thing. There is no point in having a Social Action Committee if the congregation is going to essentially divest it of the authority to function efficiently and decisively.

How do we create the right balance?

THE SOLUTION

Creating a True Partnership Between the Congregation and the Social Action Committee

One way to address this challenge is to consistently inform the congregation of what the Committee is doing and adjust decisions based upon congregational feedback. Even so, the operational decision-making must always remain the Committee's province.

While it may be true that Unitarian Universalism is the best kept secret of American religion, we should seek to avoid a situation in which the best kept secret of the congregation is its Social Action Committee. The congregation needs to be aware of what is being done in its name. And it needs to invest in those initiatives, both emotionally and financially, or they will be nothing more than feel good token gestures or a sore spot.

I would submit that the first step in doing this is to publicize to the congregation that the Social Action Committee is undertaking serious endeavors to achieve demonstrable social justice. The Committee needs to show the congregation that this is not fluff and feel good rhetoric. It is something tangible and important.

The growth of the Social Action Committee and the congregation is synergistic: flourishing in one means vibrancy in the other. Outreach can be a source of free advertising to publicize the congregation's good works and ministry to potential new members. Just like the Religious Education program, the Social Action Committee can be a critical entry point for such new members.

By way of illustration, imagine that a mom with a small daughter hears about the Religious Education program. A little neighborhood boy, with whom her child has been playing, attends Sunday classes. Her little girl wants to go too.

The next Sunday, between early morning piano practice and an afternoon soccer game, the mom brings her daughter by to check things out. The mom has no intention of becoming a vital and connected part of the congregation. That is not why she is there.

The mom was probably raised in a more traditional religious setting and ultimately drifted away for one reason or another. She has been doing quite well without attending organized religious services, thank you very much. If you asked her why (not that anyone in her life would), she would tell you that she sees organized religion as out of touch with the day-to-day realities of running a household and keeping a job. She watches the evening news and sees that the root cause of almost every war has a religious underpinning. She perceives organized religion as impractical, and worse yet, clueless regarding the pressures of living as an American in the twenty-first century.

However, a part of her yearns for something more. While she cannot put it into words, she realizes that rejecting all organized religion is not an answer, so much as an accommodation, to the lack of choices available to her. There may be something out there that would satisfy her spiritual needs, but it is not within sight. Nevertheless, she has not completely closed the door; it remains slightly ajar.

Fast forward. She is waiting in the lobby for the Religious Education class to end and she sees nothing of any consequence posted on the wall, certainly nothing about its social action efforts. People half smile as they walk by. She grows bored. She concludes, in the words of Gertrude Stein, that "there is no there there."

How about an alternate scenario? The mom waiting in the lobby for her child instead sees the following:

- Volunteers escort three homeless families right past her. The parents brush snow off their coats and those of their children, as they head to the second floor where they will be housed in one of the classrooms; given access to showers and laundry facilities; and provided with toiletries, toys for their kids, help with homework and food.
- In the center of the lobby, there is a large framed picture of a women's center in a camp for internally displaced persons in Darfur. Beneath it is an explanation that the Social Action Committee, in partnership with the Unitarian Universalist Service Committee, raised $8,000 to build this women's center and staff it for one year. The center enables women to coordinate with U.N. troops so they can travel out of the camp for firewood without being raped, to bring their children to a central point for medical care and to help one another start microenterprise businesses selling beads and more to feed their families. The congregation funded the whole thing, which otherwise would not exist.
- Just next to the picture is a sign up sheet for a trip to the State Capitol. There will be a meeting with specific state Senators and Assembly Mem-

bers to support a pending bill to restore funding slashed by the Governor for family planning and cancer screening for women below the poverty line. This lobbying is taking place through the Unitarian Universalist Legislative Ministry which has become a political force Statewide for social action consistent with Unitarian values. In fact, it has become one of the only lobbying groups in the Statehouse for humanitarian values. It doesn't just protest outside the Statehouse; it lobbies inside of it. It changes the law.

See the difference? It is subtle, but definitely different. This mom might very well be a bit intrigued. She might ask a few questions. She might wander upstairs to see how the homeless are settling in. She might ask about the status of the fight to maintain funding for PAP smears for women without the means to pay for them. She might – however tentatively — begin to think about engaging in the work of the congregation. She might conclude that this place has heart. What happens here matters outside these walls.

Modern life is a cacophony of voices calling for our attention and drowning each other out. It takes something that resonates to get through. Forward leaning Social Action is Unitarian Universalism sung in the full musical scale. It can be felt as well as heard.

A parent may see all this as a reason to fit congregational life beyond just taking her child to Religious Education, not just participating until her child turns eighteen, but forever.

And, on another level, she may also see it as integral to her parenting. Our children learn by example.

What a wonderful lesson to teach a child: that you must become involved in the issues of your time; that you must commit to the larger world around you; that you are not powerless to shape that world.

Eventually, who knows? If this Mom likes what she sees, she might even become a member of the congregation. She might surprise herself and find a place in her life for religion. She has seen what is taught. Lofty ideals like peace and unfettered love are lived. A little idealism is resurrected. A life finds its place in our Living Tradition and its good works. Social Action can be the key to that rebirth.

Spreading the Word Outside the Congregation

I have attended meetings in which participants expressed revulsion to any suggestion that "marketing" has a place in Unitarian Universalism. If this religious movement truly is the best kept secret of American religious life, many seem to want to keep it that way. We deride the idea of proselytizing, seeing it as something that would degrade what is special about this religion. I share some of that concern.

However, spreading the word that we have a kinder, gentler approach to American religious life is not the same as proselytizing. It is giving people a choice. The larger world should have the opportunity to make that choice, albeit without coercion. But they cannot make that choice if they do not know who we are and what we stand for.

Social action is an obvious way for Unitarian Universalists to become visible to the larger world. It is a way of announcing ourselves to others, of taking seriously Thomas Jefferson's exhortation that, "it is in our lives, and not from our words, that our religion must be read."

A terrific example of this lies in the Irvington Schools initiative that our Social Action Committee undertook. The full history and specifics of that project will be discussed in a later chapter. Suffice it to say that we initiated a tutoring program in an elementary school in a local urban community.

From the outset, we were welcomed by the children, administration and parents. Every so often, we would get the question, "Now what is a Unitarian?" (We were once introduced as the Ukrainian Church.) But most of the time, the fact that we were from a church was all they really needed to know. In their minds, it defined us.

To my knowledge, we have not gained one member from that initiative. But we were able to introduce the Unitarian Universalist movement to dozens of people from a community where no such church exists. They might otherwise never have heard of us. Now, they may think of us when seeking partners for the good works to which they are called.

In his famous 1966 South Africa speech, Bobby Kennedy spoke of social action as creating ripples of hope. "Crossing each other from a million different centers of energy and daring, these ripples build a current that can sweep down the mightiest walls of oppression and resistance." Through social action, we create a larger community of people who owe us nothing, from whom we expect nothing. We create a community of people who Unitarian Universalists have given – in both large and small ways – a ripple of hope.

A Social Action Committee can be the cement that binds the congregation to a higher calling. It can be a vehicle to bring in new people, an engine for congregational growth.

Successful social action brings us together. It serves to create a connection between the Social Action Committee and the congregation. People want to be part of something successful, something honest and worthy of their time and effort, something with heart that promises to change the world. Successful social action is evidence that the congregation brings integrity to its spiritual endeavors, that its beliefs match its actions.

In sum, the Social Action Committee needs to fulfill its mission in concert with the congregation. It needs simultaneously to both reach out to the community and reach into the congregation, to hold out hope in both directions.

2

THE SECOND CHALLENGE

How Can We Prevent Our Social Action Committee Meetings From Becoming So Ponderous And Uninspiring That The Key Members Start To Drop Out?

We covenant to affirm and promote acceptance of one another and encouragement to spiritual growth in our congregations.

Excerpt from the By-laws of the Unitarian Universalist Association

The Pull Away From the Positive

I find it compelling that the principle quoted above does not merely recite that we are to "promote acceptance of one another." It adds that we are also to engage in "encouragement to spiritual growth in our congregations." I see this as a clear statement that we are not only to accept people as they are, but also to help them achieve growth, to find spiritual maturity. In my view, social action is the means to finding that maturity.

Our call, in other words, is not just to what we do, but to how we do it. For instance, we must be empathetic to our members' idiosyncrasies, open to their insights and gentle with one another. However, we do not have to indulge dysfunction, disorder and a host of other patterns and behaviors that derail our mission.

I have always believed in the 80/20 rule: twenty percent of the people do eighty percent of the work. However, that is a statement of what usually happens, not of what can or should happen. If our Social Action Committees are about achieving lasting change through outreach, then all hands should be reaching in the same direction. We need one hundred percent involvement by the members of our Committees. We must offer our members a way for all to participate meaningfully.

Perhaps the single greatest force preventing people from doing social action (rather than talking about it) is not a lack of viable projects or social ills. It is the dysfunction that occurs when people work in groups.

We must minimize the capacity of the group to foster unnecessary anger, resentment and dissension. We must promote cooperation. We must insist on leadership that is informed by the principle that to live our values, we must inspire others to take chances; to be open; to share insights and information; and above all, to reach out in collaboration with other organizations in the broader world. We must lead in a way that prevents negative emotions from undermining the humanity of our members. This means that we must do our best to promote confidence, a sense of purpose and drive. To do this, we must ask more of ourselves as leaders.

Just how do we do that?

THE SOLUTION

Social Action Committee Meetings Must Accord With Our Members' Busy Schedules. They Must Have a Clear Written Agenda; Start and End on Time; and Avoid Self-Serving Detours.

In Unitarian Universalism, a Minister is called to serve the congregation, not the other way around. Likewise, our lay leaders are effectively called to serve those they lead. They must do so with intelligence; they must honor their members' commitment, their humanity.

The Chair of the Committee should be the first line of defense in seeking to lift the burden from the members of the Committee of such items as scheduling and conducting meetings; shouldering the push back of congregational bureaucracy and the negative feedback from the naysayers; working to expand funding, increase interest and reduce the possibility that the Committee might fall short of its goals (and constructively framing the reality when it does).

The Chair of the Committee should protect the members from dealing with all of that; in other words, ask less of them in that regard. Only when fundamental issues of direction or policy must be decided should the members of the Committee become involved in resolving such challenges. In short, the Chair must run interference so the Committee can remain focused on the mission. For example,

- All the members of the Social Action Committee should be reminded by the Chair at least twice by email of when and where the next meeting will be taking place. The meeting should be scheduled weeks earlier and a reminder should be emailed to everyone two days beforehand.

- A four to six week interval between meetings is appropriate. That allows enough time for people to actually accomplish something to report on for the next meeting, but it is not so far off that momentum is lost.

- The Committee should agree upon an easy method for taking emergency action between meetings. The way our Committee addressed this problem was to pass a resolution that no meeting would be considered adjourned. Instead, it would be deemed to continue until the next meeting occurred. That way, if any additional business needed to be done, the same people who were present at the last meeting could be polled by email, or better yet, in a conference call, to vote on any further action that needed to be considered.

- Votes to allocate funds from the Social Action Committee budget should be fair and democratic. This is a problem since we generally consider anyone who is a member of the congregation and attends meetings to be automatically a member of the Social Action Committee. There is always the possibility that someone who has a vested interest in a particular charity might pack the meeting with friends to vote in favor of funding that particular charity. Our solution to this was to pass a resolution that in order to vote on the expenditure of funds to donate to a particular cause, a person must have attended a majority of the past year's meetings.

- The Chair must circulate a written agenda in advance of each meeting. It is critical that the attendees be aware of the items that will be addressed and in what order. The agenda also serves the additional purpose of discouraging detours in the discussion since the members know that their particular item of interest will be dealt with at a later time.

- Someone must keep written minutes of every meeting; circulate the minutes after the meeting concludes; and the members must correct and approve the minutes at the next meeting. These minutes can be circulated not just to the members of the Committee, but also to other members of the congregation who have expressed an interest in the work of the Social Action Committee. Broad circulation increases visibility. Also, minutes can provide an important tool for measuring progress over time.

- Committee meetings should start promptly, no later than five minutes after the announced time. They also must end on time. We generally have our meetings on a weeknight commencing at 7:30pm and finishing by 9:00pm.

- The meetings should be held in a space that offers the possibility of privacy. At times, the Committee may need to go into closed session, such as when dealing with sensitive topics like personnel issues. It should be able to ensure confidentiality of its deliberations when necessary.

- Meetings should never drift or become boring and unproductive. The Chair's role in leading the meeting requires a sense of whether someone needs to be urged to move along and, if they continue to nonproductively dominate the conversation, gracefully redirected. While there may be something laudable about letting everyone have their say, it can promote unproductive diversions from the topic at hand and prevent the Committee from doing its work. A lack of focus and direction by one produces boredom and disinterest in the rest. Likewise, people who see the norm of effective use of time will tend to self-regulate. They will eventually begin to abide by the group dynamic. We just need to be patient with them.

- We must resist the impulse to allow the meeting to devolve into nothing more than a discussion session, support group or social club. We Unitarian Universalists tend to intellectualize and discuss things to death. We empathize with the suffering of the world. We like to socialize with the like-minded. The bigger the challenge, the more we tend to gravitate toward focusing on restating the intractability of the problem. However, that is not a substitute for the real work of social action. The Social Action Committee must not dwell on decrying how bad things are. It must stay focused on the larger, more difficult topic of just what we will do about it. The exigencies of the dispossessed are so pressing that we cannot afford to be distracted or self-indulgent. We cannot simply stay in our comfort zone.

Social Action Committee Initiatives Must Be Short, Clear And Achievable Baby Steps in the Right Direction.

Otto Von Bismarck, the Iron Chancellor, said: "Politics is the art of the possible." I have always believed that the single greatest mistake proponents of social action make is in failing to apply this view to outreach.

What use is there in engaging in social action that is not possible? We accomplish little by having good motivation and trying hard to achieve vague or enormous and unreachable goals. If we don't accomplish the social action goal we have set, we fail not only ourselves, but the people we might have helped. Moreover, we demoralize our Committee and lose the trust of our congregation.

We need to succeed in achieving our goals. Therefore, the goals must be achievable. It sounds simple, but if that is so, why do we keep ignoring this principle? Why do we often bite off so much more than we can chew that we end up feeling beaten and discouraged or worse, ineffectual?

For example, if our social action goal were eradicating world hunger, we would inevitably fail. In the alternative, if our goal were (a) funding three local food banks with ten percent of our base budget and (b) working with the Religious Education program to have a dozen kids make sandwiches for the homeless on a specific night, we might (excuse the expression) take a bite out of hunger and succeed.

While the latter will not eradicate world hunger, neither will simply setting eradicating world hunger as a goal. The Committee's efforts will tend to reside in failure since it is virtually impossible to solve such an abstraction.

Every great issue should be dealt with one concrete step at a time. Make each step your goal and you build in the capacity for success. Our initiatives must be within our means; in other words, our budget, human resources and time commitment.

They should also be vetted. My feeling has always been that any Social Action Committee is only one scandal away from losing the trust of the congregation. From the outset, we appointed one of our members to help investigate any nonprofit entity that would receive funding from our Committee. In fact, we have not been shy about turning down requests for funding when we have no way of adequately vetting the initiative (usually because we are not given sufficient time to do so). It has become an integral part of our approach to social action.

Moreover, I would submit that we should sometimes even forgo the belief that we should stretch to reach goals that are clearly more than we can achieve. I would rather set a series of goals, each of which is <u>less</u> than we can achieve. In other words, I would rather set a number of goals that are within our capability, than set one ambitious goal that we are likely to fail at achieving. The likelihood that they will actually happen will be greater. The aggregation of those baby steps may take us much farther down the road than if we had tried to do it the other way.

This may sound counterintuitive to the goal of accomplishing the most social action possible. It is not. Slow and steady wins the race.

And that is directly related to the most important resource of all: morale. The problems of the world are so outsized in comparison to our limited resources and abilities to solve them that it is very difficult to maintain group morale. In fact, I think the consequence of failure is why so many Social Action Committees are under-populated. Most people have little desire to join and ill-defined effort, and those who do, soon lose interest in tilting at windmills. They become discouraged and immobilized by the sheer enormity and seeming insolubility of the overwhelming problems around us. "Sophisticated Resignation," the late Rev. Dr. Forrest Church called it, not a virtue but a dangerous malaise.

If we try for too much and become demoralized, we will achieve nothing. If we develop enthusiasm by achieving small successes, we will by definition accomplish far more than if we give up.

I believe that the most powerful model for social action is to start with a few small, multi-year initiatives and add one or two more each succeeding year. Over time, baby step by baby step, the Social Action Committee will grow organically into something larger, something very special: an undertaking that both grows and succeeds every year without fail.

Declare Victory and Move On

Perception is key. When the Nixon administration was considering ways to extricate itself from Vietnam, the suggestion was made that we simply "declare victory" and leave. If we strip away the cynical aspect of that suggestion, there is an underlying truth that is of value.

Perception counts for very much. When the Committee discusses its work either internally or with the congregation and its leaders, it must project a positive and energetic image. Using the example of the hunger initiative, one might describe it as a very limited undertaking in which we "had the kids make some sandwiches."

On the other hand, it also might be described as a forward leaning initiative to commit funds to feeding the hungry and mobilizing the youth group to lead the effort. We might calculate that forty meals were created by this initiative, forty meals that would otherwise not have been provided. We might describe this as living our values in a practical and energized way.

The glass can be half full or half empty. It is all in the way we describe it.

The Leaders of The Social Action Committee (In Addition To The Social Action Chair) Must Take Ownership Of The Respective Initiatives That Move Them And Commit To See Those Initiatives Through.

The principles of Unitarian Universalism rest upon a foundation of the democratic process. The Committee rests on that same foundation. It should not be autocratic. Not only does overly vesting power in the Chair limit the range of ideas and approaches to those of one person, it also tends to prevent the rest of the Committee from becoming invested in the initiatives, in owning the Committee's efforts. It is demoralizing.

Let me focus the issue this way. How many times have you been in a Committee meeting in which someone questions the group by asking, "Why aren't we giving more money to [FILL IN THE BLANK]?" "Why aren't we doing more to prevent [FILL IN THE BLANK]?"

What is the usual response? Perhaps the Chair gives perfunctory acknowledgment to the idea and moves on because, "we have other priorities right now." That is simply another way of saying that the Chair has a full plate of work implementing what he or she has already agreed to lead.

Perhaps the Chair answers that, "we already tried something like that, and it did not work." Perhaps the Chair is defensive, taking the suggestion as an implicit criticism and responding even more negatively.

What if the answer were something different? What if the Chair said, "Good idea. Why don't you lead it?"

In other words, why not stretch sideways? Instead of a top down hierarchy, why not allow the direction of the Social Action Committee to arise organically from lateral leadership?

Often Committees tend to repeat past successes by doing the same thing, the same programs, again with only slight variation. Repeating what works is a good thing, but it is not the only thing. There must be new programs and ideas added each year. Otherwise, it becomes a recipe for stagnation.

We need to be nimble. We need to be flexible. We need to innovate. That is the job of the free thinker, the person who is not overly invested in doing things as they have always been done. The challenge is to find a healthy way to be open to new ideas and innovation. That is the invitation and opportunity presented by lateral leadership.

Of course, just suggesting change is not an end in and of itself. Those who step up to lead social action initiatives need to understand that they will be held responsible for those initiatives. They will be held accountable.

As will the Committee itself. The group must rally around this ad hoc leader and assist him or her to see things through to a successful conclusion. Funding is one obvious way of doing so. Volunteering to assist is another. The new initiative should be placed on the agenda so the leader can report on the progress and solicit input, assistance and support.

The suggestion of a new, and as yet undeveloped, initiative may start as a challenge that is somewhat threatening to the existing direction of the Social Action Committee. As the Committee embraces the idea, it will weave into the overall fabric of the group. It will foster a way of being that embraces new leadership directions.

The new initiative is placed on the agenda. It is reported on. It is funded. It merges in.

We Must Not Undermine Our Lay Leaders

A Social Action Committee dies on the vine when the personal dysfunction of the members prevents the Committee from achieving its overarching goal. No one doubts that the members of the Committee are there for the right reason: to help people. After all, no one is getting paid to attend. There is no coercion.

Yet, as with everything in life, we can become our own worst enemy. We often achieve things in spite of ourselves. The car travels at thirty miles an hour, which is better than standing still. Yet, what we don't realize is that we have one foot on the brake while the other presses on the accelerator. The car could travel at sixty miles an hour if we would just stop riding the brake.

Nice people can be ineffective; well-intentioned people can unknowingly undermine the group; even inspiring people can create dissension through their passion and enthusiasm. The way we perform our social action – however effective it is in getting help to those who need it – can result in negativity that undermines ongoing commitment.

How many of us have exhibited one of the following traits in our lives? (HINT: The answer is, all of us at one time or another.)

- We cannot make our point in a straight line, inserting all sorts of extraneous and irrelevant facts along the way. We have no sense of time and cannot seem to pick up on the looks that are attempts to cue us to wrap it up.
- We are hostile. We are negative and hyper-critical. We arrive in a bad mood and let that seep out in our congregational work. As a result, we pick fights over petty issues and inconsequential slights. We see the glass half empty and are a drag on any one else's momentum.
- We are arrogant. Our ideas are the only good ones. We do not "suffer fools gladly" and are impatient and dismissive. Ironically, we may even accomplish a great deal, but it will come at the diminishment of those with whom we work.
- We are out of focus. We will agree with everything everyone says or does. We have no ideas of our own and will not lead. We thrive on being out of the limelight. We are the self-appointed audience.

I could go on, but you get the idea. These qualities in some combination and measure exist in all of us from time to time and hence, in all groups. It is just a matter of degree. When we exhibit such qualities in excess, we hold things up and can actually blow the entire endeavor apart. That is especially unfortunate when it comes to a Unitarian Universalist Social Action Committee, since there are so few UUs in the first place. How can we allow our dysfunction to undermine our organized social action?

I believe these traits can be addressed in many ways. Here are a few suggestions:

- The Chair needs to provide advance warning to people who frequently find themselves overtaking the group discussion that everyone's time will be limited. Perhaps this should be announced at the inception of the meeting. In addition, having a written agenda provides a framework for understanding what must be covered in the hour and a half we have to meet. If they cannot stay within those limits, the Chair should ask them a question. That generally derails the repetitive and meandering discourse. If all else fails, the Chair must gently interrupt, congratulate them on their progress and move on to the next speaker. People love to be praised and congratulated. Even those who enjoy the sound of their own voice will almost always stop to hear that.

- People who show hostility in Committee settings generally lose interest in coming to meetings if their hostility is not validated. We don't disagree with them; we simply acknowledge what they say (which is not the same as agreeing with it) and continue to other business. The most difficult thing for a person who shows hostility in a committee setting is to be in a group in which they consistently provoke no reaction. They generally just move on.

- People who give off an arrogant vibe (usually without meaning to) can nevertheless, accomplish a great deal of good. They can pick up the pace for the rest. They are so invested in demonstrating how smart and adept they are (often that is a correct self-assessment, by the way) that they will undertake enormous effort to succeed. In a Social Action Committee, that success generally means that people in need will be helped. Hence, I would submit that while we should do what we can to help them soften the rough edges, we must also be accommodating to some level of arrogance in those who are committed to social action. It can be a potent force for good if channeled in positive ways.

- People who are more comfortable being kept in the background can also be worthwhile members of the Committee. There is enough background work in social action endeavors – arranging the logistics for a toy drive during the winter holidays; setting up a social action-sponsored coffee hour; etc. – that they too serve an important purpose. If we honor their limitations long enough, they may even decide to step up to the next level and lead. But it must be their call; they must be invested in it. Ask them to do small, humble things and gradually build their capacity to step forward.

In short, we are not going to eliminate negative traits that can harm our pursuit of social action. The best we can do is provide a way to avoid or limit the negatives. That effort must be informed by one overall goal: to help those in need. At every point, we must ask ourselves: does this moment we are spending have anything to do with serving the needs of the dispossessed? If not, we must get past it.

3

THE THIRD CHALLENGE

We covenant to affirm and promote a free and responsible search for truth and meaning.
> Excerpt from the By-laws of the Unitarian Universalist Association

Money is the Third Rail of Congregational Governance

Mention of money is the ultimate taboo. People will discuss intimate aspects of their sex lives, their kid's congenital illnesses, their spouse's problems at work. But under only the most pressured circumstances, when there is no other choice, will people discuss their financial picture.

We seem ashamed of our association with money. It shames us that we do not have enough. It shames us that we have too much. We are ashamed of both our spending and our lack thereof. And most importantly for purposes of this discussion, even our charitable giving shames us.

How much money is necessary to fund our social
action efforts? There is no answer. Our world's need
for social action is so out of proportion to our ability to
address it that even one hundred percent of every Unitarian Universalist congregation's budget would quite
obviously be grossly inadequate.

The problem is that we start our "responsible search
for truth and meaning" from the vantage point that
when it comes to outreach, that search will be vastly
underfunded. Is that truly a responsible way of searching for meaning?

That we are ashamed to discuss money and that
we are inevitably going to underfund our social action
efforts because they are so out of proportion to the
need are just the genesis of the problem. We must add
the fact that the Board of Trustees is effectively doling
out its own money, in that its members are presumably
donating to the institution in their individual capacities.

If there is a shortfall, the Board members (and other
congregants) will be asked to donate more. That makes
congregational spending decisions complicated. Taking
the position that the congregation needs more money
to operate leads ineluctably to the possibility that the
people saying that should donate more. The subject
leads to both inner and outer conflict.

The Board also brings to its decision on how much
to fund the Social Action Committee its personal – and
often unstated –views about money. One could argue
that the most heated discussions in the typical Board
meetings are generally not about the possible existence
of God or whether a cross should or should not hang
from behind the pulpit. The subject that really gets people going is how to spend the money.

How does this play out in the realm of social action? There is a natural tendency for the Board to see the larger picture, how the funding of the Social Action Committee will affect the overall funding of the institution. Likewise, there is a natural tendency for the Social Action Committee to focus on how underfunding prevents the necessary scope of its outreach. A systemic push and pull.

Naturally, this comes to a head in the budgeting process. There is often a sense that funding outreach must take a back seat to the sorts of expenditures that keep the lights on. The Board must ensure that the mortgage is paid; that the salary checks go out; that the snow and ice is removed.

Admittedly, those fixed expenses must be a priority. But this is a religious institution first and foremost; it is not a business. Maximizing profitability is not our goal. We have a higher one, healing the world. There has to be a spiritual reason to keep the lights on.

How do we bridge this gap?

THE SOLUTION

Living Our Values Through the Budgeting Process

The best way to resolve this problem is to engage in what I consider one of the best parts of Unitarian Universalism: living our values inside our congregation. This resides in the way we choose to allocate our limited funds.

To begin with, the choice of keeping the lights on versus funding social action is a false one. We must reject that way of perceiving the issue. The goal should be working together to do both.

Easier said than done. But the effort itself is also a spiritual undertaking. It reflects the need we have to balance the spiritual and the practical in our lives. It also calls us to higher levels of generosity. It reflects spiritual maturity. It reflects life.

If this merger, this balancing, is not how the conversation is framed, it is easy for social action to become peripheral to the mission of the congregation, or worse yet, perceived as a threat to it. It becomes nothing more than a draw on resources, and those who argue for outreach get perceived as the people who are clueless as to how challenged the congregation's finances are. That very formulation – the way of seeing this as adversarial, a zero sum game, as it were – creates dissension and has it all wrong.

The relationship between the Committee and the Board becomes strained, or at best tolerated. Neither feels that the other truly gets it. The congregation as a public presence, a beacon on a hill, a religion with real life consequences, recedes.

Ironically, the Social Action Committee can exacerbate the problem when its members start discussing the fact that it is so difficult to motivate the congregation; how unfortunate it is that we did all this work and no one showed up to the program we sponsored; what a lack of energy and drive this congregation seems to have. Going negative never really helps.

So, what is the answer? Once again, it starts with the imperative that our Social Action Committees must perform practical social action to be funded in a real way. We must be able to point to actual flesh and blood people whose lives were improved in a demonstrable and effective manner by what we did. It has to be tangible.

The reading groups and lecture series; the bus trips to protest; the colored wrist bands and bows; the accoutrements of progress toward social justice, are all terrific. We all should respect and admire the commitment they evidence. I would never state otherwise.

But they lack immediacy. They do not lend themselves to a definable measure of success. How do we measure success in protesting a humanitarian crisis? How many wrist bands and bows are enough to succeed? How many reading groups?

On the other hand, we know exactly how much is necessary to keep the lights on. We know exactly how much is necessary to pay for snow removal. One is intangible and the other is not.

Forward leaning social action must be tangible. That tangibility undergirds its immediacy. It becomes definitive. The goal is in sight.

The Social Action Committee's budget request should be specific. Likewise, it must have a rock solid answer when asked how it will use that money, and more importantly, how that use will benefit others. It must make its case. Good intentions are presumed; results are not.

Funding Through the Offering Plate

Because of budgetary difficulties, many congregations have tried to fill this need by turning to offering plate funding for social action initiatives. This involves passing the plate each Sunday for some pre-announced social action cause. The concept is a good one, but like any good idea, if taken too far, it can do more harm than good. Too often, that is exactly what happens. Perpetual offering plate collections undermine the goal of properly funding the Social Action Committee. They end up, once again, allowing a congregation to ride the brake.

Nevertheless, there is certainly a logic behind using the offering plate collections to augment social action funding. Study after study has concluded that the normal plate collection for the congregation's general funding will inevitably be a far lower figure than a plate collection for a targeted, pre-announced social action cause. The increased amount collected for outreach is "found money", so to speak, an increase in the annual donation by the congregation as a whole, money that would not otherwise have come in.

On the other hand, a number of unintended consequences arise when the offering plate collection becomes the primary means of funding social action through weekly use throughout the year.

First, the amount of the plate collections may not be sufficient to address emergent social action needs. In other words, the nature of social action – when it is done in a serious way – is that it needs to have the resources to addresses sudden crises. Without a significant base budget, the Committee will be relegated to waiting for enough offering plate collections to aggregate to what is needed to help the families dispossessed by a sudden house fire; the children whose parents cannot afford to buy them basic school supplies the week immediately before school starts; the first aid support needed in a place struck by devastating natural disaster.

Second, when the plate collection is perpetual, the congregation inevitably suffers plate burn out. There is nothing special about this Sunday's plate collection versus next Sunday's. The only thing that might change is the pet project that is the topic of the solicitation. Perpetual requests for social action giving at every worship service leads to uninspired and downward trending collections.

Third, being UUs, we tend to not want to turn anyone away. Therefore, we fill the perpetual plate collections with too many pet projects. That is good in one sense since it does create versatile outreach. However, the danger is that we end up throwing relatively small amounts of money at a disjointed collection of good causes to keep everybody happy. We accomplish little we can put a finger on.

There are other ways a perpetual plate collection undermines social action funding. However, my purpose is not to reject the idea entirely, but instead to demonstrate at least one way of focusing it to better effect.

At the outset, at least half of the Social Action Committee's budget should be provided as a lump sum line item in the congregation's overall budget allocation. That will allow the Committee to respond to emergencies and give it a basic amount of funding for the Committee's programs and donations. This will also keep the main activity of the Social Action Committee from devolving into perpetual fundraising.

Additionally, any social action offering plate collections should be limited and focused, both in number and in scope. There are many ways to accomplish this. In Summit, we have arrived at one method. It may not work for everyone, but it is what seems to work well for us.

We have three plate collection groupings spread out through the fiscal year dedicated to three unrelated social action projects. Each grouping involves four successive Sundays, constituting a total of eight plates in each grouping (because there are two services per Sunday).

Each grouping of four Sundays follows the same pattern, which has become a formula for us now.

- On the first Sunday, we explain the initiative in detail, setting out a specific financial goal that we want to achieve by the fourth Sunday.
- On the second Sunday, we reiterate the nature of the initiative and why it is important.
- On the third Sunday, we give specific figures on how much has been collected through the halfway point and by what percentage we are under or over fifty percent of our goal.
- On the fourth Sunday, we explain how much has been collected in the three previous Sundays, and we make a full court press to have the members of the congregation increase their donations so we will either achieve or exceed the goal. In other words, we enlist the congregation as a fully informed participant in making the goal a reality. Indeed, the week after each plate collection concludes, we report back to the congregation on whether we met or exceeded our goal and by what percentage. We declare victory in this team effort and move on. We work together with the congregation, not at cross purposes to it.

The nature of the three annual social action projects is key. We stay away from goals that might be viewed as pet projects of someone on the Social Action Committee. Instead, we choose projects that will have a broad appeal to the congregation as a whole.

By way of example, in 2010 our first set of three plate collections for the fiscal year took place in September with the stated goal of creating an emergency fund for sudden social action needs. Of the money we collected, we donated several thousand dollars immediately to the Unitarian Universalist Service Committee's initiative in Pakistan. There had been reticence from certain segments of our culture to donate to Pakistan because of all the bad press it received in the so-called Global War on Terror. The need for our funding was pressing and emergent. One-fifth of that country was underwater due to heavy flooding.

The second set of plate collections took place in November to fund one year of transitional housing for a homeless family through HomeFirst. That organization (originally called the Interfaith Council for the Homeless of Union County) is one of the preeminent charities helping to house and advocate for the homeless in Northern New Jersey. Our congregation has a strong bond with HomeFirst since we were one of the houses of worship that started it in the first place.

The timing of the plate collection was not coincidental. It took place just as winter was approaching. It coincided with our congregation housing homeless families in our facility to live for three weeks during the Thanksgiving and Christmas holidays. We often have a family present at one of the services to kick off the collection. We also have the Executive Director of Home First speak at another of the four Sunday services.

By way of background, while the congregation had always generally supported HomeFirst financially, when I first took over as Chair, our Social Action Committee

wanted to come up with an additional initiative. It would
be one that was consistent with our principle of setting
a specific and attainable goal to achieve a measurable
result. So, instead of just raising money for HomeFirst's
general funding, we opened a dialogue to craft a specific goal for that funding. We arrived at the idea of pay-
ing for one transitional housing unit for a year.

Such a unit provides a family with the stability of living in an actual apartment of its own for up to a year
to set down roots in the community by becoming gain-
fully employed; sending their children to the local
public school; and otherwise becoming a productive
and active member of the community. These units are
"transitional" in the sense that the family must move out
within the year (usually with a variety of assistance from
HomeFirst). However, the fact that the family has this
housing and HomeFirst's surrounding social programs
without cost gives them breathing room to achieve
the stability to plan to re-launch themselves into the
world.

The annual cost for one such unit is approximately
$15,000. We have been able consistently to collect at
least $7500 from the plate collection, which we match
from our Social Action Committee budget for an aggregate donation of $15,000. Our HomeFirst offering col-
lection has gained vitality with each succeeding year. In
2010, we collected approximately $11,500, which when
added to the matching funds of $7500 from our Social
Action Committee budget, aggregated to $18,500. Thus,
we collected far more than our $15,000 goal.

Another set of four plate offerings takes place in Feb-
ruary. It is usually a collection for an international issue
of social concern, and the money is donated to the Uni-

tarian Universalist Service Committee. There is a later chapter in this book dedicated to our partnership with UUSC. The basic idea is that we pick a topical UUSC initiative that is definable and will cost exactly the amount of our four-week collection goal. It is always something that will resonate with the congregation. In 2011, it was a collection to feed, clothe, house, and educate 20 Haitian schoolgirls for one year. The project took place at Camp Oasis in Haiti, a secure location for children to attend school without the threat of the lawlessness and violence that is ravaging parts of that country. As will be detailed later in a later chapter, we greatly exceeded our goal. This was especially important since the Unitarian Universalist Congregation at Shelter Rock provided a triple match for what we collected.

We do not split our twelve Sunday offering plate collections (three sets of four) into twelve different funding initiatives. We believe that would dissipate their effectiveness. Instead, we set three specific grouped goals that we can meet or exceed.

In a word, we focus. By doing so, we make our offering plate collections special. By doing that, we increase the amount of money collected because we don't overdo it. We use the specific projects as leverage to promote a higher order of magnitude of social action giving. It is an opportunity for our congregation to live its values in big ways.

Directed Donations

Occasionally, our success has led members to give us funds donated on the condition that they be used for a specific purpose. For bookkeeping purposes, they are generally segregated from the general funds of the congregation in some manner, usually by creating a separate general ledger allocated account.

Just as is the case with the offering plate collection, directed fundraising is another example of something that can transform a Social Action Committee for the better. It is also an example of an approach that, if handled without clear purpose, can become its downfall. It must be handled with care; less is more.

The advantage of a directed donation is obvious. It is money that can be utilized by the Social Action Committee above and beyond its approved budget, literally "found money". It can energize an otherwise dormant initiative.

For example, each year, a couple from our congregation donates a sizable amount of money for our Social Action Committee to feed the hungry. This effort began after a series of articles in the local paper about how the shelves of the local food banks were bare.

That donation was the basis for an initiative led by one of our Social Action Committee members who had already devoted an extraordinary amount of effort to help the homeless and hungry in our community. Through this additional funding, we have become a significant funding mechanism for a number of food banks in Union and Essex Counties. Many hundreds of people have been fed with food purchased through those directed funds. Very few people in our congregation even know that this directed donation was made (though, of course, the Board was informed), much less who made it. It is truly an example of members in our congregation who live their values without fanfare.

On the other hand, directed donations can become destructive to a charitable institution, as well. Hunger is one thing, but what if someone offered a directed donation to press for stricter immigration laws or welfare reform? With a few adjustments, one could imagine ways of presenting those ideas that would not be inimical to UU values. But what if the Social Action Committee did not want to pursue such projects?

It could refuse the money, but what if those funds represented a high proportion of the total funding available to the Committee that year? It would be like a starving man being offered food he does not particularly care for. Does he refuse it?

Directed donations can serve to divest the Social Action Committee from having control of its own initiatives. Who would want to serve on such an impotent committee? How could such an approach be empowering?

Moreover, if a large percentage of the congregation started diverting its general donations in favor of directed giving, the Board might begin to fall short of having enough funding for basic needs. In essence, directed donations can also divest the Board of its proper role in deciding how to allocate congregational funds. It takes the decision on big picture items away from the people who presumably see the big picture (the Board) and gives it to people who generally do not (individual donors).

The bottom line is that directed funds must be unexpected, welcome aberrations. But the basic funding for the Social Action Committee must arise from the congregation's budget in combination with a limited (rather than perpetual) offering plate collection. The Social Action Committee should welcome directed donations when they happen but not go out of its way to encourage them.

Other Forms of Fundraising

I would be remiss if I did not mention some other forms of fundraising that seem to have worked for us in Summit. I am the first to admit that we have not yet utilized them to their fullest potential. They are still works in progress.

Dances and communal meals have been particularly effective since they are relatively low cost and serve to bring out both active members and those that are not. Indeed, the best fundraisers are those that are attended by unfamiliar faces.

A few of our Social Action Committee members recently organized a Halloween Masquerade Ball to raise money for the Legislative Ministry of New Jersey (more on that later). It was a tremendous success. Another of our members organized a Friday dinner for the same cause, which met with similar success. I am convinced that we can do more with that type of approach.

Summit also fundraises for general funding through a vibrant communal garage sale and at a later point in the year, a services auction. While we do not dedicate those funds to social action, other congregations might find that a useful way for funding such initiatives.

The point is that the offering plate and directed donations are not the beginning and end of the potential methods to raise money for social action. The possibilities are endless.

Bad Bookkeeping Can Break a Social Action Committee

If the funding for the Social Action Committee is limited to a base budget, the bookkeeping is rather simple. A fixed number is allocated to the Committee at the beginning of the fiscal year and every expenditure simply subtracts from it. At the end of the fiscal year, the number should be zero. As a matter of sound accounting practice, non-profit organizations are not generally permitted to carry over general funding from year to year.

However, if the funding is a combination of a base budget; a variety of directed offering plate collections; directed donations by individual members of the congregation; and possibly ad hoc fundraisers for specific initiatives, the bookkeeping can become very complex.

This complexity presents more than merely a boring mathematical discussion. The Social Action Committee, and ultimately the Board, has an obligation to spend funds in accordance with the purposes for which they were collected. In other words, if we collect money for HomeFirst, we cannot spend it on a UUSC Africa initiative.

The only way to keep everything straight is to employ a bookkeeping protocol that is thorough and accords with sound accounting practices.

There are many ways of doing this, but my suggestion involves four steps. They are:

1. The congregation's bookkeeper should be asked to maintain ledgers for all committees and email the applicable ledgers to the committee chairs monthly. Email ensures that the information is timely. The ledgers should clearly show every withdrawal and the reason for it. The ledgers should also show the balances available to the committee on a monthly basis, in the manner set forth below.

2. The Social Action Committee should have two general ledger ("GL") accounts, one for the base

budget and one for the directed funds (fund-raisers, dedicated donations, etc.). However, the directed GL account should have sub accounts that clearly state the nature of the money that is deposited in them: e.g., Legislative Ministry, UUSC projects, HomeFirst, etc.

3. The committee Chair or her designee should be the sole person allowed to approve expenditures from any of those accounts. The formal check request should reflect which account the money is coming from by GL account and subaccount so there is no confusion. The sole exception should be that any check request reimbursing the Chair must be co-signed by another committee member and any allocations from one GL account or subaccount to another should be co-signed by the congregational treasurer.

4. No checks or other expenditures should be distributed to anyone from Social Action Committee funds except by the Social Action Committee Chair or her designee. Among other reasons, there is usually a cover letter that should accompany the check putting the payment in context. If it is sent by someone else in the congregation without the Chair's knowledge the letter may not say what it should. Moreover, the Chair will not know the check was cut and sent.

This all may sound like a rather complicated system, but actually, it is far less confusing than the alternative of jumbling all the funds together or separating them in some arcane way that is largely inaccessible to oversight.

Spending the congregation's money wisely involves understanding what money is available to be spent and why.

Perhaps in the final analysis, that is what this entire dialogue between the Social Action Committee and the Board must be about if they are to achieve anything meaningful together. It must reflect shared priorities and the shared commitment to achieve them.

The Unitarian Church in Summit (UCS) receives the 2010 Unitarian Universalist Service Committee's (UUSC) Social Action Award. Pictured left to right: Charles Huschle (UUSC Senior Associate for Individual Giving), Gary Nissenbaum (UCS Social Action Chair) and Rev. Vanessa Rush Southern (UCS Parish Minister).

The Sanctuary of The Unitarian Church in Summit.

Left to Right: UCS Social Action Committee member, Kelly Vis-
conti, meets with UCS Youth Minister, Rev. Emilie Boggis.

Left to Right: UCS Director of Religious Education, Tuli Patel,
UCS Social Action Committee Member, Joe Parsons, UCS Social
Action Committee Chair, Gary Nissenbaum, UCS Social Action
Committee member, Ted Brewer.

Left to right: UCS Social Action Committee Members Stephen
Jackson, Karen Jackson and Mia Morse.

Left to Right: UCS Social Action Committee member, Brian Halpin and UCS 2010/2011 Board President, Thomas Howard.

Left to Right: UCS Social Action Committee Members, Kimi Nakata, Jean Crichton, Lorraine Wearley, and Kathryn Werlein.

Rev. Nicole Kirk, UCS Acting Assistant Minister.

Left to Right: UCS Social Action Committee member, Peggy Kreider and UCS Social Action Committee Chair, Gary Nissenbaum.

Left to Right: UCS Social Action Committee members, Martin (Marty) Rothfelder, and Carolyn Baldacchini.

Left to Right: UCS Social Action Committee members, Dean Nielsen, Jennifer Nielsen, and Martin (Marty) Rothfelder.

4

THE FOURTH CHALLENGE

How Can We Prevent Local Outreach From Being
Undermined By The Enormous Scope Of The Need?

*We covenant to affirm and promote justice, equity and com-
passion in human relations.*

Excerpt from the By-laws of the Unitarian
Universalist Association

If we Try to Solve All the Problems that Surround Us, We Shall Inevitably Fail.

Our faith does not require us to solve all the problems that surround us. Instead, we are simply urged to
"promote justice, equity and compassion in human relations." We have to respect the distinction between solving and promoting.

There are two basic outcomes when people try to
solve all the social ills surrounding them. Either they
quickly become burned out, which leads to dejection
and giving up, or they see the task as so overwhelming
that they don't even try, which leads to dejection and
giving up.

How many of us were idealistic when we were younger, before the real world intruded? Why is idealism the province of the young?

I would submit that it is a major mistake to try to solve all the ills confronting the world. It sounds good but leads to a very bad place. Ironically, we end up doing less for those in need because the magnitude of the problems they confront discourage us.

However, people in need cannot just walk away as we can. They have no other lives to go back to, no distractions of wealth and power to keep them occupied. Recognizing the social ills of the world is not a choice for them. They are confronted with those social ills everyday.

So the challenge is to stay the course even though we start out so far behind and we know that in the end, we cannot have a clean win. We need to find a reason to make an effort that will always fall short of solving the need. We need to define success differently.

But what is that definition?

THE SOLUTION

Social Action as a First Step

According to Lao-Tzu, "[a] journey of a thousand miles begins with a single step." My answer to this challenge is that we need to take a first step forward in our local community.

Few would argue with the premise that we should first address the needs of those struggling in our immediate community. We often know some of the folks personally. It is almost always an easier "sell". But how do we choose a place in need of our social action efforts?

The answer: throw a stone in any direction. That place needs our social action efforts. Now turn around and throw in the other direction. That place needs our social action efforts too.

We are immersed in an ocean of social need. Even if the stone we throw lands in an upper class community, there are all sorts of social action needs. Often, they are just generally better hidden. How many of those privileged communities are populated by battered spouses; alcoholics; pain medication addicts; suicidal adolescents; and depressed senior citizens? Social action is not the exclusive province of the financially needy. (On the other hand, the financially disadvantaged may actually work in such communities and be a vibrant part of their social fabric, notwithstanding the fact that they cannot afford to live there.)

We need to start somewhere. I would submit that the most obvious first approach would be to find a resource-challenged community and determine how to become a meaningful part of that community's life without making things worse. We must ask ourselves how we may best follow the injunction of the Hippocratic Oath to first, do no harm.

For purposes of illustration only, I would offer our Irvington Initiative as an example of how to create an appropriate entry point. Again, I want to stress that this initiative is not the last word in outreach. It is merely an example of how our congregation stepped in. It was what worked for us.

When I took over the Social Action Committee, my partner suggested that I concentrate my efforts on starting an initiative in Irvington, a particularly challenged community only two towns over from Summit (which is one of the most affluent communities in New Jersey).

The township of Irvington is adjacent to the more widely-known city of Newark. Although Newark is similarly challenged, it has had an extraordinary renaissance over the last two decades. Unfortunately, Irvington has not received the resources with which Newark is blessed: an airport, government offices, performing arts center, flourishing business district, busy port and overall national prominence. Irvington's challenges were far less mitigated.

My partner put me in touch with Mayor Wayne Smith of Irvington, who she happened to know. It must have been strange for him to take my call and to hear me explain that I was from a suburban church that had no creed, that welcomed everyone, even atheists and that we wanted to come into his town and help.

It wasn't just the typically awkward discussion about how we represent a religion that is unlike what most people consider a religion. I had the added burden of explaining that we wanted to help, but did not know exactly what we wanted to do. Most of us in Summit only knew Irvington as an exit on Interstate 78 that we passed at high speed on the way to Manhattan.

To his credit, Mayor Smith did not hang up the phone. Instead, he took the time to help me focus on what we might do together. Since I had just taken over the Social Action Committee, I was unsure how much backing I would receive from the congregation. So, I suggested an initiative that I could do alone, if need be. I wanted to dip my toe in the water, so to speak, to start small so that if this all became a fiasco, we could learn from our mistake and move on without embarrassing anyone. I did not want to start my tenure as

Chair of the Social Action Committee with a public failure.

Being the managing principal of my law firm, I am in charge of hiring. It occurred to me that with New Jersey's high unemployment rate, some people in Irvington probably had a need for someone to review or even help write their resumes. It was something bite-sized that I could do myself.

I proposed that the Social Action Committee conduct a resume writing seminar in the local Irvington library at which we would literally write the resume of anyone who showed up and also teach them how to use the Internet to search for a job. The mayor agreed that it would be a good start.

On that first night, I loaded my car with an office computer, printer, blank paper and a bunch of diskettes (remember those?) and set up shop in a room in the back of the library. I was joined by four other members of our Social Action Committee.

We jointly presented a PowerPoint® on how to use various employment websites. We then split up to draft resumes and cover letters for each of the ten men and women who attended. One of the more interesting aspects was the range of backgrounds of these Irvington residents. There were mid level executives who had been laid off from telecommunications companies, teachers and even a physician who had just immigrated to this country.

We performed three weekly sessions. At the conclusion, everyone was given multiple hard copies of the resumes and individualized cover letters we had drafted for them. They were also each given a diskette so they could edit those documents later, as circumstances warranted.

The word got out among our congregation that we were engaged in something interesting in Irvington, and people started gravitating to assist. Our resume writing seminar started to move in unanticipated directions. It was my first introduction to how our congregation would continue to consistently step up to support and enhance our Social Action initiatives.

In fact in the later sessions, we were joined by a number of members of our congregation who had had no involvement with the Social Action Committee before. One of them happened to be affiliated with Dress for Success®, an organization that helps people lacking sufficient resources to obtain appropriate clothes for interviews and professional positions. She joined our last session. She offered to help anyone who needed a suit for an interview.

The number of Irvington residents attending kept growing. By the last session, we had over fifteen people. They even decided to create their own employment support group that kept on meeting on its own after our seminar concluded.

Something was in the air. As Pastor Basil King of Christ Church in Cambridge, Massachusetts said over a century ago, "Go at it boldly, and you'll find unexpected forces closing round you coming to your aid."

We reported back to our congregation by including a short article in the newsletter and giving a brief summary at the beginning of a Sunday service. I considered this one of the most critical aspects of the initiative: garnering support among the congregation at large by

involving them, even virtually, in the success of the initiative.

People started to approach me about becoming
more involved in the nascent new direction of our Committee. I believe that the fact we succeeded (albeit, with
a very modest initiative) started to give us credibility.
It reminded me of the oft repeated advice on giving a
speech: Tell them what you are going to tell them. Tell
them. Then tell them what you told them. The analogy
to social action is to tell the congregation our goal for
the initiative. Succeed at it. Tell the congregation that
we all succeeded at it.

And move on to the next one.

At about this time, our Minister, Rev. Vanessa Rush
Southern, gave a powerful sermon that people still
speak about years later concerning the deplorable state
of our inner city public schools in New Jersey. The basic
thrust was that this was more than just an issue of funding budgets and motivating teachers. It was nothing less
than a humanitarian crisis of the first order. Our children were being divested of their right to an education.
As Unitarian Universalists, we needed to do something.
In fact, she gave examples of what other Unitarian Universalist congregations had already done. Where was
Summit in this mix? When would we step up?

One of the members of our Committee was moved
to action. He discussed with Vanessa and me whether
there was something the Social Action Committee could
do in Irvington to help its students.

I contacted Mayor Smith, who had actually stopped
by at one of our resume writing sessions to see how
things were going. I told him that we wanted our next

initiative to involve the school system. He referred me to a particularly well-functioning elementary school called the Chancellor Avenue School.

When the Social Action Committee discussed this, as usual, Vanessa viewed it as a teachable moment for us. She explained that the wrong way of doing it would be to go the school and tell the principal what we had in mind. The better way would be to show some humility and basic respect by asking them what role they might want us to play[1].

I am convinced that following her approach was the key to the ultimate success of this initiative. The first series of meetings with the school set just the right tone. Ultimately, the principal asked us to start a tutoring program in reading and math that would take place for six consecutive Wednesdays in the Fall and again, in the Spring.

Our member who had proposed the initiative took the lead in organizing and implementing what came to be known by our congregation as the Irvington Initiative. He was able to harness the unusually deep bench of our generally highly educated congregation to have the program supported, among many others, by members who were working teachers and supervising administrators (including a District Superintendent) from other school systems. In other words, the volunteers who performed the one-on-one tutoring with the kids were generally overqualified for the task.

A striking example of this was one of our other members who holds a Ph.D. degree in education. He is a retired official with the World Bank where he implemented and evaluated educational programs in Glo-

---

1   She also wisely suggested we bring food to the initial meeting. Never a bad thing.

bal South countries. He was asked by the Social Action Committee to become the "community member" of the Chancellor Avenue School Leadership Council after the principal suggested that the church provide some-one for that slot. In that role, he ultimately brought an entirely new dimension to the initiative, offering his services to review and analyze Chancellor Avenue School's scores on the New Jersey ASK (Assessment of Skills and Knowledge) Test, a standardized examina-tion that assesses the scholastic progress of elementary school students.

He prepared an elaborate spreadsheet using the scores to identify specific areas that would benefit from tutoring. With that data in hand, the principal created a special after-school tutoring program to help at-risk students improve their NJ ASK performance, a pro-gram for which the Social Action Committee contrib-uted additional tutors. Another of his analyses showed that the tutoring contributed to the school's greatly improved test results in 2010, especially in Math. This success led us to renew our commitment to the new principal's after-school tutoring program in 2011, with a particular focus on reading skills.

There was definitely a spiritual side to this initiative. One of the seven principles of Unitarian Universalism is to "affirm and promote justice, equity and compas-sion in human relations." The Irvington Initiative was clearly in accord with that principle since it enriched our understanding of our neighbors – literally, since they were only two towns over from Summit – living in this challenged community.

Most of us had little or no contact with such com-munities, so our understanding was informed by the stereotypes in the media. For example, the media promotes the concept of inner city unemployed people on welfare who are too often untrained and uninterested in working. Our resume writing project demonstrated the very opposite: their professional backgrounds were varied and often accomplished, and they wanted a job just as badly as anyone else out of work.

Another example of a stereotype promoted by the media was that the parents of kids in our urban schools are disinterested in their education. In fact, we were impressed by how many parents would not only bring their kids to our evening tutoring sessions at the school, but also would stay for the entire two hours watching us tutor their kids. Many of them worked with the tutors in such activities as teaching the children to solve reading and math puzzles and play word games. They would do so after long days at work with little time for themselves. Moreover, we were welcomed with open arms by the local PTA which was very much in favor of this initiative.

I found this all the more impressive given that none of the parents seemed to have a clue as to what a Unitarian was. They knew nothing of our liberal faith; our commitment to require no creed or religious dogma; our roots in American history. They only knew that we were a group from a local suburban church that wanted to help their kids. That was enough. They trusted us.

We also had tremendous support from the school administration. After the terrific job the principal did helping to launch our program, he was transferred. We were fortunate that his replacement was just as enthusiastic. She personally attended the evening tutorial sessions; purchased pizza for the kids; and saw to it that everything kept humming along. She also helped organize, and participated in, the after-school tutoring related to the NJ ASK test. Her upbeat disposition and welcoming manner served to rapidly solidify our nascent ties with the Chancellor Avenue School. Ultimately, she was transferred as well, but again, we are fortunate that a principal who is passionate about working with us took over. She has been extremely supportive and open in helping to continue our involvement with the school.

The point is that once again, the stereotype the media portrays of challenged urban school districts having principals that are selfish and out of touch, who neglect the interests of the kids and fail to cooperate with parents and others who want to improve education, was simply not borne out by our experience. The principals kept changing, but they were all uniformly enthusiastic and helpful in making the initiative a success, notwithstanding the fact that it involved their working with us after hours, on their own time. Against all stereotypes, they have created a highly functional school with a serious learning atmosphere.

As usual, our congregation as a whole was incredibly supportive, as well. We invited the Mayor to give a presentation to our congregation, which over one hundred members attended. The tutoring was attended by dozens of members, many of whom were new faces. Once again, this initiative was so accessible that it was also a magnet for people who otherwise had not found their place in our congregation. It was an opportunity to breach the fourth wall, for the audience to come on stage and be part of the story.

The member of our Social Action Committee who led this effort was nothing less than a force of nature. He was (and continues to be) tireless in organizing and improving the initiative each year. I am convinced that this effort would have foundered without his energy, intelligence and tenacity in making it a success.

A number of the other members of our Social Action Committee also played an important part in enhancing our burgeoning relationship with Irvington. We routinely asked the people we met in Irvington what they needed from us (once again, as opposed to foisting upon them what we thought they needed from us). From that ongoing discussion, a range of additional Irvington initiatives sprouted, including:

- Chancellor Avenue School gave us a wish list of items they needed, which our congregation provided, including musical instruments, audio visual equipment, computers, printers and books. We ultimately obtained all of these items for them through a series of solicitations of the congregation.
- We conducted a series of vocational presentations for Irvington high school students enrolled in the "Career Ambassador" program.
- We conducted a parenting workshop.
- We conducted a Tai Chi stress reduction class for the teachers.
- We provided food baskets for the December holidays for those families that might not have enough to get them through.
- We conducted a winter coat drive for the kids.
- Our Religious Education program conducted computer seminars for senior citizens.
- We conducted a lactation class for expectant mothers.

Our congregation had initiated a true partnership with our Irvington neighbors. It continues.

Local Emergencies: Social Action That is Responsive

Another way we took steps locally came about when the recession of 2008 started to overtake our country, there were articles about local food banks in Union and Essex counties not having enough food to stock their shelves. It was something that had been completely unanticipated and largely unheard of. The traditional challenge facing food banks was being understaffed or underfunded. In this area of the country, it was unusual to have so little food to give out for such a sustained period.

We immediately raised this problem at our Social Action Committee meeting. The decision was made to allocate a portion of our budget to donating to local food banks and pantries.

One of our members with a background in working with the homeless and hungry volunteered to handle the initiative. Consistent with our policies, his first task was to visit the various food banks and pantries to determine which should receive our funding and in what proportion. This was part of the vetting process.

As usual, the member leading the Hunger Initiative not only took his leadership of that initiative seriously, he went beyond his initial charge. He started to utilize our Religious Education program to help make, and distribute, sandwiches for the homeless throughout not just Northern New Jersey, but also parts of Manhattan. Another of our members organized our congregation to help serve meals to the homeless through an organization called SHIP (Summit Helping its People). Our congregation had been involved with SHIP for many years, and our two members built on that relationship to transform our Social Action Committee's Hunger Initiative into something far larger than it otherwise would have been.

As previously mentioned, an integral part of that organic process within our congregation involved at least three anonymous members who made directed donations for our Hunger Initiative. Collectively, the funding came to nearly seventy five hundred dollars. When coupled with money from our existing base budget, the Hunger Initiative took on its own momentum, which continues to this day.

Stepping Out of the Way: Honoring the Congregation's Existing Initiatives Outside of the Social Action Committee.

There is a natural tendency for a Social Action Committee to seek exclusivity in its mission within the congregation. Indeed, in the abstract, it does not serve the congregation's interest to have a dozen separate committees serving social action causes. There can be duplication of effort; wasted resources; and lay leaders can be stretched too thin.

However, a centralized approach to social action can also have major downsides. We are obviously a volunteer organization which cannot thrive if people are prevented from undertaking social action that they feel is important. If they do not want to do so through the traditional committee structure, is that a legitimate reason to discourage them?

Our Social Action Committee welcomed every interested person who wanted to join. However, if a member wanted to form his or her own project regarding a particular issue without our involvement, we were also supportive.

This resulted in a number of important initiatives that functioned outside our Committee, such as

- creating a Centennial Committee to raise $100,000 in cash and in kind for local and international social action efforts in celebration of our congregation's one hundred year anniversary;
- advocating for affordable housing in Summit, something our congregation has been integral in fighting for throughout New Jersey;
- working with Habitat for Humanity to build homes for those in need;
- working with Planned Parenthood and its affiliates;
- creating a Racial Justice Task Force;
- undertaking a Green Vespers service to celebrate and honor our congregation's commitment to the environment;
- creating a memorial by our Moving Toward Peace Committee that included colored ribbons hanging from the front of the Church honoring the soldiers and civilians who were wounded or killed in Iraq and Afghanistan; and
- supporting the establishment of a Department of Peace in the executive branch of our federal government.

And the list goes on. This approach is not indicative of chaos or disorganization. I see it as a vital demonstration of our diversity as a congregation.

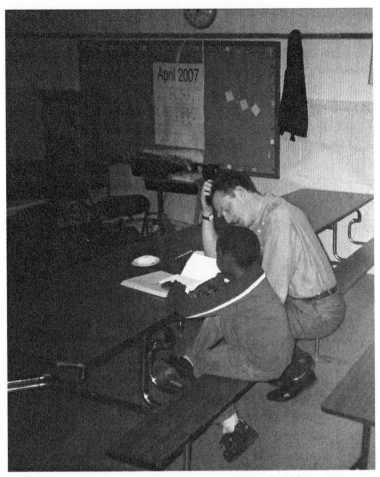

UCS Social Action Committee member, Wim Sweldens, tutors a
child at the Chancellor Avenue School in Irvington, New Jersey.

The Irvington Neighborhood Improvement program in which the
UCS Social Action Committee gave out school supplies to children whose families could not afford them.

The UCS Social Action Committee worked with the Irvington Neighborhood Improvement Program to give out school supplies to children whose families could not afford them.

Students at the Chancellor Avenue School in Irvington, New Jersey, participate in the UCS Social Action Committee tutoring program.

UCS Social Action Committee member, Brian Halpin, leads the UCS contingent for Spruce Up Day at the Chancellor Avenue School in Irvington, New Jersey.

5

THE FIFTH CHALLENGE

Does A Religious Institution Have A Legitimate Place In Politics?

We covenant to affirm and promote the right of conscience and the use of the democratic process within our congregations and in society at large.
Excerpt from the By-laws of the Unitarian Universalist Association

Does Unitarian Universalism Belong in the Political Arena?

The initial protection afforded by the First Amendment is that "[c]ongress shall make no law respecting an establishment of religion or prohibiting the free exercise thereof." Simply put, our constitution generally forbids the government from insinuating itself into religious life.

For many of us, the reverse should be discouraged, as well. We believe that religious institutions should not insinuate themselves into political life. That may not be a constitutional issue, but it is a sense many people have that it is not a good thing to blur the lines between the two.

Problems often arise when a congregation has a dominant political viewpoint. There is the very real possibility that members with the minority view will feel excluded. This may result in their keeping silent when others express political views that "of course, we all agree with."

It is a not a long leap to imagine such members deciding to simply withdraw from the congregation entirely because they feel unwelcome. And generally, the rest of us will never know why they withdrew. We will never have an opportunity to make amends.

How can we pride ourselves in not having a religious creed when so often, certain members of our congregation feel that we have a political creed? We need to ask ourselves whether we want to require our congregants to pass an implicit political test to be accepted by the rest of us. If not, then why do so many of them feel they must do so?

How do we fix this?

THE SOLUTION

The Social Action Committee's Role in the Political Debate Must Be Limited to Advocacy that Comports with Unitarian Universalist Values, Not Endorsement of Candidates or Parties.

When I speak to groups on behalf of the American Civil Liberties Union of New Jersey, I am amazed at how few people realize that it does not endorse political candidates or parties. It is an advocacy group, not a political action committee. It supports causes, but does not endorse the people or party espousing them.

Likewise, the Social Action Committee should never endorse a candidate or political party. It must strictly limit its involvement in the political debate to issues that clearly comport with Unitarian Universalist values, not to personalities or political parties. It must advocate.

Unitarian Universalism has played a long and vital role in advocacy. One of the early casualties of the 1960s civil rights demonstrations in the south was Unitarian Universalist Minister James Reeb, who was killed by segregationists during the 1965 march in Selma.

That sort of personal protest against racism in America is still a vital part of Unitarian Universalism. However, still more is necessary. We need to advocate for all of our Unitarian Universalist principles by utilizing the democratic process in society at large.

In the modern era, for better or worse, that means lobbying. Many issues of public policy directly implicate our UU values. We must not only speak truth to power from outside the halls of government, but we must also insist on a seat at the table when legislation is being considered to address those issues. To quote our Unitarian Universalist principles, we are asked to "affirm and promote ... the use of the democratic process ... in society at large."

Statewide Advocacy Networks

One of the most compelling developments in Unitarian Universalism nationwide is that the Unitarian Universalists in at least fifteen states have formed respective Unitarian Universalist Statewide Advocacy Networks. One such network is in my state of New Jersey.

An Advocacy Network is a joint effort of some or all of the Unitarian Universalist congregations in a particular state that wish to collectively advocate for Unitarian Universalist values in the public arena. Each Advocacy Network undertakes the responsibility to organize the Unitarian Universalists in that State to educate the public and take action on issues of public policy. In many states, it also creates a corresponding entity to lobby with respect to pending state legislation and executive action by the Governor or his agencies. Many also appear *amicus curiae* (friend of the court) in pending court cases with significant public policy implications.

The various advocacy networks coordinate with one another under shared leadership. They also work with the Unitarian Universalist Association and the Unitarian Universalist Service Committee.

In New Jersey, fifteen of the state's twenty-one UU congregations recently formed an advocacy network known as the Unitarian Universalist Legislative Ministry of New Jersey ("Legislative Ministry"). The Legislative Ministry represents over 90% of Unitarian Universalists in our state.

The Legislative Ministry also works with a related organization called the Public Policy Network. The latter was organized to engage in the actual lobbying activities in regard to legislation implicating Unitarian Universalist values in New Jersey. The Legislative Ministry is run by an Executive Director who reports to a Board of Trustees made up of representatives of a number the participating UU congregations.

The Legislative Ministry has four issue task forces: (a) Health Care; (b) Affordable Housing/Economic Justice; (c) Environmental Justice; and (d) Emerging Issues (for example, Marriage Equality and Immigration). Individuals from member congregations may join one or more of these task forces. One of the purposes of the task forces is to review proposed legislation and recommend that the Public Policy Network advocate to support, object to or revise legislation. They also work with the Network to organize petition drives; collaborate with other advocacy organizations; and disseminate information on issues as they relate to UU values.

The Role of the Social Action Committee in Working with an Advocacy Network

One might ask why it is necessary to have an Advocacy Network. Why not have each UU congregation advocate independently on issues?

The answer is that, on a number of levels, religious institutions are not set up to do so. First, while the Internal Revenue Service provides deductibility of donations to religious institutions, that status is not absolute. If the institution engages in substantial political activity, it can risk losing its nonprofit status.

Indeed, the standard formulation for a charitable institution that wishes to sponsor advocacy work is to create both a purely charitable organization under section 501(c)(3) of the Internal Revenue Code and a separate entity for political lobbying and advocacy under Section 501(c)(4). Thus, the organization will operate on two parallel levels: its tax deductible 501(c)(3) entity and its non tax deductible 501(c)(4) advocacy entity.

The second reason is that there is power in numbers. Unitarian Universalism is a comparatively small religious movement. Our numbers alone will not impress local state legislators. We need to make our voices heard through organized, grassroots lobbying efforts and other methods of communicating in a way government is likely to hear.

A couple of years ago, two of our members were appointed to the Steering Committee of the nascent Legislative Ministry of New Jersey. Our Social Action Committee provided some of the seed money to get it off the ground through one of our sets of Sunday offering plate collections.

Now that it is functioning, one of our other members is our congregation's liaison. She also chairs the Legislative Ministry's Healthcare Taskforce. Another of our members chairs the Affordable Housing/Economic Justice Taskforce. They both report to us at each of our Social Action Committee meetings on the status of those respective initiatives. They also coordinate fundraising for the Legislative Ministry within our congregation and serve on its Board.

Each of these members is a point person for getting the word out to our congregation about the important work of the Legislative Ministry. They have labored tirelessly to communicate that the Legislative Ministry is functioning; being heard; and needs our support.

By its very nature, an Advocacy Network rises or falls based upon the support of its member congregations. For this reason, it is imperative that each congregation have participating liaisons who continue to solidify those ties.

The Rationale for Promoting a Partnership between the Social Action Committee and the Advocacy Network

The importance of the Advocacy Network to the overall goals and objectives of the Social Action Committee is clear. Social action is about creating <u>lasting</u>

improvement in the treatment of people in our society. Talking about it, while important, is only a start. The laws, regulations and court cases that continue to exist after our words fade away must reflect our humanity.

Free speech can sometimes sound like a cacophony of noise emanating from the aggrieved and maligned, the powerful and the entrenched. But it is nevertheless, the "sweet sound of democracy." At critical junctures, when Unitarian Universalist values are implicated, our voice needs to be heard above the din.

6

THE SIXTH CHALLENGE

SINCE THERE IS SO MUCH SOCIAL ACTION LEFT UNDONE IN OUR LOCAL COMMUNITIES, WHY SHOULD WE DIVERT ANY OF OUR FOCUS TO INTERNATIONAL CONCERNS?

We covenant to affirm and promote the goal of world community with peace, liberty, and justice for all.
Excerpt from the By-laws of the Unitarian Universalist Association

Why Should We Divert from Our Important Local Outreach Efforts by Addressing International Concerns?

Since taking over as Social Action Committee Chair, the relatively few complaints that have reached me have almost all questioned why we were diverting our resources to international outreach when so much needs to be done locally. When I point out that the majority of our funding is spent on local initiatives, these critics are not convinced. This concern is raised again every year.

They raise a legitimate point. If every community in the world engaged in outreach to those in its local area, there would be no need for social action to cross borders. Yet, we are confronted with the reality that wealth is unevenly distributed in the Global South[2], as is the capacity for social action. Moreover, the help that religious and other charitable organizations do provide to the low-income (or no-income) people in the Global South is often withheld from the people who need it most. Dictators and oligarchs open Swiss bank accounts while their people search in vain for potable water and basic pediatric health care. Likewise, local ethnic differences can also mean that one tribe or sub-community is favored by those in power when aid is being distributed.

But the question remains: why should we divert our Social Action Committee resources from people in our local communities who desperately need it in favor of people a world away who also desperately need it?

Why should we engage in international social action?

THE SOLUTION

Living Our Lives as a Statement of Conscience

Spiritually based social action is concerned both with the impact on those who are helped as much as the impact upon those who do the helping. We cannot ignore international suffering because to do so would be an implicit assertion that suffering within our borders is more important than that outside our borders; that our tribe is more important than theirs; that they are the other, the lesser. That statement would degrade our spirit. It would contravene our religious commit-

---

2   Global South is essentially the modern term for what used to be called the Third World.

ment to a faith that directs us "to affirm and promote the goal of world community with peace, liberty, and justice for all."

As Peter Singer wrote in his groundbreaking article, "Famine, Affluence and Morality[3]," local suffering in the Global North pales in comparison to the extreme suffering in the Global South. We are compelled to care for those we will likely never see or know. We must expand our compassionate imagination beyond the familiar, the comfortable. As Singer states, it makes "no moral difference whether the person I can help is a neighbour's [sic] child ten yards from me or a Bengali whose name I shall never know, ten thousand miles away".

So, we help people in Africa, Asia and Latin America because in doing so, we make a personal statement about what sort of people we are striving to be. We make a statement of what Unitarian Universalism stands for. We make a statement that is worth hearing.

Partnering with the Unitarian Universalist Service Committee

How do we best accomplish international outreach? As challenging as it is for a Social Action Committee to engage in outreach within the local community, it is much more difficult to play a useful role in an international project involving social justice. The latter presents far greater challenges.

As previously stated, it is possible that money donated internationally will not reach its intended recipient due to a lack of government infrastructure or corrup-

---

3   P. Singer, "Famine, Affluence and Morality" *Philosophy and Public Affairs*, vol. 1, no. 1 (Spring 1972), pp. 229-243 [revised edition]

tion. Likewise, while many international aid projects have some worthwhile purposes, the means of achieving those goals are not always consistent with Unitarian Universalist values. A good example is the Global Gag Rule, a federal law that bars nongovernmental organizations that accept United States foreign aid from using the money to assist in funding or counseling related to abortions.

The further from home we send our funding for social justice programs, the more ways it can go astray. Our Social Action Committees operate on the basis of trust; the congregation trusts that we will use the money we are given wisely. If that trust is undermined — even through no direct fault of our own — the damage to that relationship can be severe. The loss or diversion of money sent to a distant place in need can result in such damage.

Our Social Action Committee has addressed these concerns by partnering with the Unitarian Universalist Service Committee (UUSC) for most of our international initiatives. UUSC is a nonsectarian organization that advances human rights and social justice in the United States and around the world. Guided by Unitarian Universalist values and the Universal Declaration of Human Rights, UUSC partners with those who confront unjust power structures and mobilizes to challenge oppressive policies. It is affiliated with the Unitarian Universalist Association (UUA), but operates as a separate entity from it.

UUSC's efforts were begun by Waitstill and Martha Sharp, a Unitarian minister and his wife who went to Czechoslovakia in 1939 to help Jews and others living there escape. They started these efforts before the Nazi invasion and continued them for five months thereafter, all the while risking arrest and worse. They eventually returned to the United States, but in 1940, they made their way into occupied France to continue their work. Later that year, they returned to the United States for good, having helped over 2,000 people escape Nazi occupation. UUSC has since offered assistance in a wide variety of humanitarian crises and social-justice challenges worldwide.

The strength of partnering with UUSC is that its initiatives are quite obviously consistent with Unitarian Universalist values. Further, its reputation is beyond reproach for fairly and effectively utilizing the funds donated for humanitarian goals. It often partners with grassroots groups to get where it is needed quickly and efficiently.

Yet, it is my contention that, with some notable exceptions, UUSC is being undersupported by individual Unitarian Universalist congregations. Much of the time, congregational fundraising for UUSC is limited to Guest at Your Table boxes of change begun the Sunday before Thanksgiving (as important as I believe that is). Too often, with the exception of active lay leaders and the minister, the congregation seems to be only vaguely aware of the existence of UUSC and what it does.

I would submit that if one of the key challenges for the Unitarian Universalist movement as a whole is to address its relatively small impact on American religious life in comparison to that of other religions, it is incumbent upon the movement to explore every legitimate avenue to project itself onto the larger stage. This is especially true in regard to having an impact on social justice. In essence, we need to make our efforts count. Partnering with UUSC is one of the best ways of doing so.

All of this leads to the next question: how should a small to medium congregation partner with UUSC? I submit that simply fundraising to give an annual donation in support of UUSC is only part of the answer. Remember, the idea is leverage. Social Action Committees need to partner with UUSC in furtherance of their joint social-justice mission. Giving general funding is only the beginning — we need to do more.

A New Approach to Partnering with UUSC

Social Action Committees should lead a two-pronged approach within their congregations. First, they should be an advocate with their Board of Trustees to ensure that a significant portion of the congregational budget is allocated for a direct donation to UUSC. The second piece should be for the Social Action Committee to pick a particular UUSC initiative and use the offering plate to fundraise for it.

These two prongs serve different purposes. The donation from the congregation's budget is a defined sum of money being provided to an undefined cause. By that I mean it is a donation that is unallocated and directed to UUSC's general funds. The rationale is obvious: the very nature of UUSC is to address unanticipated humanitarian emergencies. It must have a pool of general funding that will allow it to shift its resources as necessary.

The second approach involving the offering plate, however, is allocated and directed to a specific UUSC project, rather than to general funds. Notably, this does not raise the previously discussed problem of donors directing their donations to projects they want a nonprofit organization to initiate. UUSC presents the congregation with a choice of three to five of its existing initiatives. The congregation chooses among a list already approved by UUSC. Every project on the list is in need of funding.

As discussed in an earlier chapter, a typical congregation will inevitably donate less money to the offering plate if it is going to a general appeal than if there is a specific narrative — a story, if you will — accompanying the solicitation. By participating in a specific project, we encourage the congregation to see the relationship with UUSC as a vivid and vibrant partnership.

I should add that this partnership between the Social Action Committee and UUSC does not preclude a partnership between individual members of the congregation and UUSC. We also need to encourage our congregants to join UUSC directly and participate in supporting its causes with individual initiatives.

A Step-by-Step Practical Approach to Partnering with UUSC

The approach that our Social Action Committee has taken to working with UUSC — one of many equally legitimate approaches — is that we ask UUSC for a list of projects that are appropriate for offering plate funding. The key is to pick a project that is tangible and will effectuate international social action. To better ensure success, the funding necessary should be just under the amount expected to be collected in the particular set of offering plates. (But every so often, we might also want to take a leap of faith and try to collect more than we think we can.)

For example, in 2009, our Social Action Committee opened a dialogue with UUSC in which we learned that it was seeking to construct 10 women's centers in the camps for internally displaced persons in Darfur. Each would essentially be a large Spartan structure, with just four walls and a roof, in which the women of the camps could gather; obtain medical care for their children; coordinate their forays outside of the camps to gather firewood with the U.N. Peacekeeper patrols; start microenterprise businesses to feed their families; and so forth. In essence, they could begin to rebuild a community for themselves.

It was estimated to cost $8,000 to both construct each center and staff it for one year. The goal was to ultimately construct ten. UUSC and its partner in Darfur had only built two.

Our Social Action Committee decided to fund the construction of a third. We made this our goal for a grouping of four successive Sunday offering plate collections. We invited representatives of UUSC to come to our congregation to present a slide show of what was going on in Darfur and why the women's centers were such a vital part of addressing the deteriorating humanitarian crisis there. As an added bonus, they also arranged for us to be visited that day by a woman from Darfur who was working directly with UUSC on the project. By the fourth Sunday, we had collected the $8000 necessary to build the center.

In 2010, we turned to Uganda. UUSC had an oxen project in which a donation of $500 would purchase one ox. That may not sound like much, but in that part of the world, a working ox could be shared by families to till their soil for food and to rent to other villagers for a modest income. This was especially important since so many families need to replace oxen killed or lost in the civil wars that have ravaged Uganda.

Once again, we invited UUSC to give a presentation on the initiative. Over four Sundays, we collected more than $7,000 from the offering plate. Some of the funds were even donated outside the offering plate by one of our members directly after the UUSC's presentation.

By any measure, that plate collection was a success. UUSC calculated that our donations would buy enough oxen to sustain 119 people. Those were 119 people in Africa who did not go hungry and began to rebuild their lives, because of the efforts of a Unitarian Church in Summit, New Jersey.

I cannot emphasize enough how important it is to make these international initiatives tangible to the congregation. While we were collecting for the Uganda oxen initiative, there was a concerted effort to pass legislation in that country making homosexual conduct punishable by draconian prison terms, even execution. It was reported in the media that there was a group of American Fundamentalist Christian leaders whose preaching precipitated this effort.

On the third Sunday of our appeal to the congregation for the oxen initiative, we made the point that the only thing many Ugandans knew about American religious leaders was that they abhorred homosexual behavior. This made it incumbent upon Unitarian Universalists to show Ugandans that there was another side to American spiritual values, a side that wanted to help feed their hungry children and make things a little bit better for their war-torn population.

There was a clear uptick in the money collected the Sunday we made that appeal. It anchored the initiative to our congregation. It resonated. And it led to more starving children being fed a world away.

Our 2011 offering collection for the UUSC-sponsored project in Haiti is an example of the power of stretching beyond what one might think is possible. UUSC challenged us to meet the goal of raising $8,520 for Camp Oasis, a pilot project in which schoolgirls in Haiti would be provided with living quarters and a program of education and extracurricular activity analogous to a boarding school. Importantly, Camp Oasis also would provide security for their basic safety and access to healthcare and social services to help them recover from the trauma of the earthquake and its aftermath.

We made the case to the congregation through e-mail blasts and the newsletter as to why this was important. Again, we were visited by a UUSC representative who gave a slide presentation about the project. We also read a letter from the pulpit from the director of Camp Oasis acknowledging our congregation's efforts.

We had been hesitant to set $8,520 as our goal, since we had not raised that much in our previous two UUSC projects (Darfur in 2009 and Uganda in 2010). However, we decided to stretch.

To our surprise, we surpassed the $8,520 goal in the first three Sundays. The fact that the solicitation happened to coincide with the television reports about the one-year anniversary of the earthquake clearly helped. So little had been done, and our congregation had a ready means to assist. I also believe that the visit by our UUSC representative was an important part of our success.

By the fourth Sunday, we had collected over $11,800 for an $8,520 project. There would be an additional 3:1 match from the Unitarian Universalist Congregation at Shelter Rock. Therefore, the total provided for the initiative would be well over the $40,000 threshold to fund the entire Camp Oasis pilot project.

Although there is a rationale for seeking to collect slightly less than we think is possible (to ensure success), there is also a countervailing rationale for seeking to stretch beyond what we think we can accomplish. There is always the possibility that we can do better than we think we can. Where there is life, there is hope.

A women's center in a Darfur refugee camp constructed with
funds raised in 2009 by The Unitarian Church in Summit (UCS).
This is one of ten centers that the Unitarian Universalist Service
Committee and its partners are seeking to fund and construct in
the refugee camps. The women use the centers to create a community in which they can provide for their children's basic healthcare; share food and supplies; and (as pictured) start microenterprise businesses to provide an income for their families.

Oxen grazing in Uganda purchased by the UCS in 2010 through a project spearheaded by the Unitarian Universalist Service Committee and its partners. The oxen were shared by families to till their soil for food and to rent to other villagers for a modest income. This is especially important since so many families need to replace oxen killed or lost in the civil wars that have ravaged Uganda. The UCS was able to fund a sufficient number of oxen to sustain 119 people.

In 2011, the UCS funded a project spearheaded by the Unitarian
Universalist Service Committee and its partners to build Camp
Oasis, a pilot project in which schoolgirls in Haiti are provided with
living quarters and a program of education and extracurricular
activity analogous to a boarding school. Importantly, Camp Oasis
also provides security for their basic safety and access to healthcare
and social services to help them recover from the trauma of the
earthquake and its aftermath. The amount collected by the UCS
greatly exceeded its initial goal and was tripled by a matching grant
from the Unitarian Universalist Congregation at Shelter Rock. The
total provided for the initiative was well over the $40,000 threshold
to fund the entire Camp Oasis pilot project.

7

THE SEVENTH CHALLENGE

How Do We Empower Our Members To Take The Social Action Committee In New Directions Without Engendering Chaos?

We covenant to affirm and promote the respect for the interdependent web of all existence, of which we are a part.
> Excerpt from the By-laws of the Unitarian Universalist Association

The Needs of the Many

Social outreach can sometimes resemble herding cats. Everyone comes to the Social Action Committee meetings for their individual reasons, which may or may not dovetail with the group's priorities. They each have their own views, whether or not articulated at the meetings, about how outreach should be done. They each have a list of what they would change, given the chance.

And who is to say they are wrong? There is no one right way of doing this sort of work. In fact, as previously stated, I believe it is critical that Social Action Committee members be empowered to voice their concerns and possibly move things in a different direction. That can be healthy, a sign that the Committee is flexible and nimble.

We live in a world in which children go hungry; political dissenters are tortured; and money warps the line and structure of our democratic institutions. The vast majority of people are not disinterested in the larger issues of our day; they are demoralized by their inability to engage those issues in a meaningful manner. They hunker down and guard their small slice of the pie and pray, not for a better world, but just to be left alone, to dodge calamity for one more day.

Our Social Action Committees must gather such people and empower them to lead in the direction their hearts mandate. We must help them soar.

Hence, while the basic function of the Social Action Committee is to engage locally and internationally, its higher purpose is to provide a spiritually empowering experience, to foster spiritual maturity. It must allow its members the freedom of thought and expression to find their humanity by helping humanity. It must provide not just teachable moments, but teachable years. It must encourage spiritual growth.

All well and good, but there is a fine line between that and the outright chaos that can ensue if everyone is marching to the beat of a different drummer. The challenge is how to structure things so that individual initiative does not undermine the mission or momentum of the group.

How do we achieve the right balance?

THE SOLUTION

Allowing Social Action Committee Initiatives to Grow Organically

The answer is that the Committee should encourage its members to step forward with suggestions for new initiatives that they will volunteer to lead. As previously stated, these new initiatives should not undermine or duplicate existing ones. If they do, there should be a full and frank discussion of whether the two are capable of being conjoined. In other words, can they be modified to blend together?

We must create an overarching structure for the Social Action Committee that serves as fertile ground for individual initiatives within that larger structure. Using this model, the Social Action Committee can grow organically. Each initiative that it undertakes can be led by a different member who continues on the Committee from year to year. Over time, the Committee will pick up new members along the way who come up with their own initiatives that also continue year to year. Developing that momentum creates a vibrant and growing Committee.

Listening to the Unheard Voices

I have always felt that the point at which a Social Action Committee moves from being an important part of the congregation to being an essential one is when it consistently attracts members whom no one has heard from before, when it moves beyond the usual suspects.

In a practical sense, a Social Action Committee can encourage this result by doing the following:

- When new faces come to a meeting, everyone in the room should be given an opportunity to introduce themselves to the group and to speak (briefly) about why they are attending.
- No acronyms without explanation. The Chair should slow the conversation down when it gets too heavy with references to the UUA, UUSC, UULMNJ and the Seven Principles. Also, discussions of a pending initiative should be accompanied by a brief introduction explaining the history of the initiative and the reason it is being discussed.
- Whenever a new person attends a meeting, the Chair should make reference to the fact that everyone at the meeting has an open invitation to propose an initiative they would like to lead, so long as it is consistent with UU principles and not duplicative of an existing initiative. Visitors should be made aware that they can step up any time the feeling moves them. There are no impediments.
- The visitor should be placed (with their permission) on the Social Action Committee email list. The Chair should seek him or her out and obtain feedback as to what the experience of the meeting was like. We should make visitors feel welcome.

An Example of Organic Growth

Last year, I was approached by one of our members concerning a New York Times article that referred to immigrants, accused of violations of one sort or another, who were being held in local New Jersey prisons while awaiting a hearing on their status. This was contrary to Federal law and regulation which mandated that such persons be held in civil, rather than criminal, detention.

The conditions were deplorable. They were not able to interact meaningfully with family or counsel; not given adequate health care, nor access to basic items such as pillows and toiletries. She asked if there was something the Social Action Committee might do to address this.

We promptly made her the head of our Immigration Initiative; provided her with modest funding; and asked her to point us in the direction she thought we should go to address this important issue. Since the plight of undocumented immigrants going through the indignities of the administrative hearing system is something that is not well-publicized, part of her task involved educating the rest of us. She brought a speaker from First Friends, an interfaith group that visits and supports detained immigrants, to speak to our Committee and circulate literature.

Around this time, there was a presentation from the pulpit concerning the inhumane aspects of our nation's immigration policies. In the course of that service, she announced that she would be convening a meeting of her taskforce afterward.

Half the people who later attended that meeting were not involved with the Social Action Committee at all. Some of them, we had never seen before.

Essentially, she had reached outside the set of familiar lay leaders to become an entry point for people who would not otherwise have stepped forward. She grew our Committee organically.

Organic Growth That is Nimble

Another example of promoting organic growth beyond the functional occurred a couple of years ago through our connection with the Township of Irvington. In mid-August, we received a call from Mayor Smith's office. The town had a program to provide basic school supplies – pencils, pens, notebooks, etc. – to children whose families did not have the means to purchase them. The town was having difficulty funding and staffing the program that summer. We were asked if we could purchase the supplies and help distribute them within one week, the week before school started.

This situation highlights many of the principles discussed in earlier chapters. First, because our funding was not tied exclusively to the offering plates, we had access to the several thousand dollars from our base budget necessary to buy a sufficient amount of supplies. Second, because our Minister, Board of Trustees and Finance Committee were supportive of the Social Action Committee, we were able to obtain immediate email authorization to proceed. Third, because we had built bridges to members of our congregation performing social action outside of the Social Action Committee, we were able to enlist the support of our congregation's Centennial Committee (a group that was raising $100,000 in our congregation's 100th anniversary for social action causes).

Within days, fifty boxes of supplies were delivered to the distribution site in Irvington. Our people went there to help give them to the lines of waiting kids.

Having a social action structure that is nimble, clearly understood and trusted both inside and outside the congregation made the difference.

8

MY PERSONAL JOURNEY: BECOMING A UNITARIAN UNIVERSALIST

I believe that the path I took to becoming a Unitarian Universalist was not unique. However, for that very reason, my journey may be useful for understanding how we can attract new members to our congregations. More precisely, it might help illuminate how our Social Action Committees in particular can become entry points for such folks. While growth is not an end in and of itself, it can be a critical ingredient to energizing social action outreach. Outreach applies on two levels: we reach out to those we help and to potential new members.

In 2003, a friend introduced me to the Unitarian Church in Summit. I had been raised in a different religion. However, eventually, we all need to learn that we cannot allow others to make spiritual decisions for us. Not making waves or upsetting a great aunt is ultimately an inadequate reason to remain cleaved to childhood religious training. We must choose for ourselves because we are the ones who must live with that choice. And we must die with it, as well.

By that time, I had drifted away from organized religion. However, the alternative of no religious affiliation had clear drawbacks. While I could accept the reality that I would never find a spiritual home with people who believed as I did, I was not sanguine about giving up on such a possibility for my child.

At the very least, I believed that religion was particularly important in three specific life transitions: birth, marriage and death. I was unhappy that my child would go through those – and possibly other – life passages without a spiritual home to embrace him.

So, at the suggestion of a friend, I attended a Unitarian Universalist service at the Unitarian Church in Summit. It is housed in a magnificent structure in the center of downtown Summit, New Jersey. Its architecture is that of a classic New England Congregational Church. The inside, painted with soft yellow and white trim, bursts with sunshine, giving one a sense of openness and optimism. On the day I attended my first service, kites hung from the balcony. I gathered that the service was to be about kites.

Our minister, Vanessa Rush Southern, who recently described herself to me as "a six-foot-tall red head", gave a poetic and warm sermon about how our lives are like kites, sailing high, colorful and filled with unexpected delights, as the wind buffets us about. Yet, we must also be tethered by that kite string, lest we fly away completely. So far, so good.

The next service I attended celebrated the life of Billie Holiday. The congregation had hired a performer to sing her songs. Between each number, Vanessa and other speakers made reference to personal struggles that this African American singer (and others of her era) had to endure. Vanessa spoke about how Billie Holiday had confronted racism, for example, by singing the anti-lynching song, "Strange Fruit", to all white audiences. That sort of thing.

To be in a place that assumed love at the heart of the universe and good at the core of humankind was liberating. The service about kites was not really about kites. It was a metaphor for the search for meaning in the ephemeral. Likewise, the service about Billie Holiday's songs was not about those songs. It was about the troubling intersection of celebrity and race in American history. Our culture elevates celebrities to quasi-royalty, but at least in those days, if the celebrity were African American, they would also be perceived as the lesser. Ultimately, the service was about the need for simple fairness and respect in how we treat one another.

Of course, this subtle, searching and strongly intellectual approach is not the only way to communicate a meaningful spiritual message. Certainly, many people need heavy-handed guilt to motivate them to spiritual commitment. But it was the best way to communicate such a message to me.

Thinking about that, I realized that if this medium and message resonated with me, it was highly likely that others drawn to the congregation might be kindred spirits. Perhaps I would find that since we had all essentially self-selected this place of worship, we might be of a similar mind on many other matters. Perhaps I was surrounded by people cut from the same cloth as I.

I brought my son to the next service. It happened to be the Coming of Age ceremony, a service for kids a bit older than he. It is a ceremony akin to a Communion or Bar Mitzvah in which a twelve or thirteen year old child assumes the role of spiritual adulthood. Being Unitarian Universalists, the ceremony is structured by the kids themselves, culminating with each making a statement to the congregation about his or her individual spiritual/religious beliefs.

The service began with the theme music from Star Wars. Actually, it was more subversive than that. It was the evil Darth Vader theme music from Star Wars.

After a few skits about Unitarian Universalism, each of the kids stood one by one and gave statements about their spiritual views. I happened to be sitting next to an older woman who was obviously not part of the congregation, but instead, a family member of one of the children.

The first young man began with, "Do I believe in God?"

My neighbor muttered softly to herself, "Well, of course you believe in God. We're in a church."

As if on cue, the young man in the pulpit answered his question with, "No, I do not."

He explained that for him, God was for the weak-minded. People who had intellectual integrity would admit to themselves that there is no God and that when we die, we are simply gone.

Next, a young woman stated that she did not believe in God as an old man with a white beard, but instead believed that God was the sum of all of us.

It went on like that. What struck me most was that not one of the dozen or so kids repeated exactly the views of the others. Each had his or her own religious belief.

When they were done, Vanessa spoke again, with words that just grabbed me. She said we acknowledge what each of you has said as your own truth. But what is also true is that what you believe at the age of twelve will not be the same as what you believe at the later stages of your life. And, as you change your views — and then change them again — we will be here for you. That is what it means to be part of this congregation. We commit to being on this religious journey and adventure together.

I had never heard anything like that in a house of worship. It was bursting with intelligence and humility. And it was dead on true.

But the story continues. After the service, my son agreed with my suggestion that he enroll in the congregation's religious education program. It so happened that he was just the age for what is known as the OWL program, short for Our Whole Lives. It is a curriculum that goes beyond a typical school-based sex education course. While offering straight answers to the biology of sex and ways to prevent STD's, the program also deals with how to have a healthy sexual relationship; it takes away the mystery and misguided assumptions about the LGBT (Lesbian, Gay, Bisexual, Transgender) lifestyle; it uses the medical realities of sexuality as the beginning rather than the end of the discussion.

To learn more, I met with Carole Haag, our congregation's then Minister of Religious Education. She is a slight woman with short gray hair, an energetic smile and a warmth that fills the room. Through her, I had an encounter that redoubled my commitment to Unitarian Universalism.

I asked her what the OWL program was about. She explained the nuts and bolts to me, adding that one of the more compelling aspects of the program was the nature of the questions that the kids asked during the discussion at the end of each class. She said, a boy might ask, what does it feel like to be inside a woman?

"That's quite a question," I said.

"But, Gary, it is an understandable question, isn't it? I mean isn't that something a boy would want to know? Shouldn't we give him an answer to that?"

It was certainly not an answer anyone had given us growing up. Here was a religious leader telling me, in the most matter of fact way, that she got it. She understood the things that reasonable adults understand after the sometimes unfortunate diversions of childhood religious training.

It was not just what she had said, but what resided beneath those words. Her message was not limited to sexuality. It had to do with something far larger. Here was a religious leader who would take care not to crush my child's spirit as he grew into manhood. My child would not need to struggle to attain healthy attitudes toward sexuality in spite of religious doctrine. She was telling me that she would get this right.

Religion without the need to reject. Religion that gets it. A truly 21st century approach. I was through the looking glass. I had arrived where I belonged.

9

A SEARCH FOR MEANING THROUGH SOCIAL ACTION

Joining the Unitarian Church in Summit at that time was part of a progressive shift in my outlook. I had come to believe that the midpoint of my life was behind me. I had a sense that as bad as it would feel someday to be dying, it would feel a lot worse to be dying with regrets. I had done very little charity in my life. Although it was true that I had helped people in need from time to time, I had never involved myself in a sustained non-profit venture. How could I justify that to myself at the end? Wouldn't that be my major regret someday? As Horace Mann wrote, "[u]ntil you have done something for humanity, you should be ashamed to die."

I reached out to several local charities. I was surprised to find that very few charitable organizations are set up to provide a meaningful role for volunteers who call from out of the blue. That amazed me because I had two decades of legal experience in complex commercial law. I was willing to offer my services *pro bono*.

Yet, none indicated an interest in my services (though donations would be welcome).

There was one exception, the American Civil Liberties Union of New Jersey (ACLU-NJ). It treated my inquiry as an opportunity rather than a bother. It committed to assign a case to me, notwithstanding the rather shocking news that the ACLU-NJ had far more volunteer attorneys than cases to hand out. It took a full year before I was assigned a case (suing to obtain information about a Homeland Security project that required local law enforcement to identify ill-defined "potential threat elements" in the community).

I eventually became a public speaker for the ACLU-NJ and a member of its Board of Trustees. It was (and still is) very meaningful working with that organization. I believe that future generations will look back on the early 21st century and view it as a time of particular crisis for civil liberties in this country. The ACLU and all of its state affiliates are fighting the battle of our time. I am proud to be a part of that.

In addition, I decided to form my own non-profit. It was called the Community Business Development Foundation. Its purpose was to train budding entrepreneurs in the depressed urban areas of New Jersey to start a business. We were certified by the Association for Enterprise Opportunity to teach a six week microenterprise course that would take the person through every aspect of starting a small business.

By the time they graduated from the program, we would have helped them complete a formal business plan. That would be submitted to an internationally-recognized micro lender, with which we worked, to fund their business.

Microenterprise has been wildly successful throughout the Global South. However, with some notable exceptions, it has not caught on in America. The reason is obvious. Given the easy credit available (up until a few years ago) to even the most financially-challenged Americans, there was little incentive to go through the microloan process. Moreover, the microenterprise course that we taught was essentially a stripped down version of an undergraduate business and marketing course. If somebody was serious about taking such a course, they could easily enroll in a local community college.

Neither of those factors are present in the Global South. That is the reason microenterprise has become so popular there and (again, with some notable exceptions) not here.

We had a number of people enroll in our program, but only one completed the course. She was a woman originally from Haiti who quit her job at a telecommunications company to pursue her dream of starting a catering business.

She did all the homework assignments we gave her. We helped her set pricing; create menus; edit the content for her website; and more. When she graduated, we had a small get together at my law firm to celebrate. When we gave her the certificate of completion, she burst into tears.

Her business thrived. She served the local urban communities of Newark and Irvington. She eventually became so successful that she was able to open a storefront catering business in Irvington.

Where she was murdered.

We worked with the family to set up a reward. We met with local law enforcement and tried to work with the Essex County Prosecutor's Office. Ultimately, her killer was not apprehended for one overarching reason: no one in the neighborhood would cooperate with the police. We were told informally that since the murder had been committed in daylight at her business location, there were a number of surrounding business owners who were well aware of who had done this. But the "no snitching" policy prevailing in that community prevented anyone from working with the police. So, the killer went free.

I ultimately closed down the Community Business Development Foundation. But I did not give up on Irvington, not by a long shot.

The Indian Ocean Tsunami

The day after Christmas 2004, one of the largest natural disasters in modern times struck Indonesia and surrounding countries in the form of a tsunami. When I attended services that day, it was all over the television and radio.

I was shocked that no one said a word about this tragic event during the service (run by a guest minister). At the end of the service, there was time set aside for the congregants to give "the last word." I made the point that there had been a tsunami and suggested we might address this tragedy in some fashion.

There were expressions of concern, but as the week progressed, no one followed up with a fund drive or collection for the survivors. Ultimately, I told the President of our Board of Trustees that I was donating money to UUSC to assist in rebuilding from the devastation.

I expressed my disappointment that our congregation was not already in gear on this issue, but if he wanted to start a collection for UUSC, I would assist.

I later learned the reason we had not had an immediate collection. For one reason or another, the Social Action Committee no longer existed. It had lost its members. We were in the paradoxical situation of being one of the largest Unitarian Universalist congregations in New Jersey and likely one of the few without a Social Action Committee.

Unbeknownst to me, our President spoke with Vanessa and our Assistant Minister, Emilie Boggis, about how I seemed to have some interest in social action. He suggested they consider me to revive the dormant Social Action Committee.

Vanessa invited me to lunch. She broached the possibility of my taking on this responsibility. I responded that if I were to do so, I would propose the following approach:

- We would undertake small, bite-sized social action projects, each with a clear beginning and end point. We would set out the goal and afterward, measure if it had been achieved.
- We would empower our members to take on leadership roles for specific projects that moved them. With the Committee's support, we would hold them accountable for moving those projects forward to a successful conclusion.
- We would be supportive of others in the congregation who performed social action witness through book readings, protests, workshops, lecture and so forth. If they needed our assistance

(such as in publicizing those events), we would gladly give it. However, generally speaking, those items would be done outside of our Committee. They would not be our focus.

- We would treat one another well in good fellowship. We would strive to maintain a positive internal dynamic as we set about the challenge of healing our world.
- The Committee would decide on its own projects.
- Vanessa and Emilie would need to have our back as we transitioned. We would need their ongoing support to smooth the way if we inadvertently stepped on any toes in our good faith effort to remake our congregation's social action effort.

Vanessa heartily agreed with that approach.

And so it started.

When I mentioned to people in my congregation that I was writing this book, one asked why it was necessary. Isn't it simply setting out best practices of sound business management applied to the realm of a volunteer organization in a religious institution?

Of course, the answer is yes. However, that answer does not detract from the need for this book. I am hopeful that it will help address the complaints I have heard from other social action chairs about (a) a listless Committee that talks things to death and cannot get out of its own way; (b) a sense of futility in facing the enormity of the ills of society that demand social action; (c) backbiting and gossip among the Committee members; (d) a lack of funding; (e) an offering plate collection that is unfocused, devoid of enthusiasm and unsuccessful; and (f) a lack of leadership.

I wrote this book to provide a guide for how to begin to correct some of those dysfunctions. However, I repeat that what we have done in Summit is a work in progress. It is by no means perfect. In fact, many UU congregations throughout the country are much larger than we and have a far more robust social action component. We have simply found a way that works for us, and some of what we have done may work for others.

Unitarian Universalism has all the elements necessary to inspire bold and effective social action. It is non-hierarchical, allowing the lay leadership to set the congregation's direction; it is unafraid of growth from within; it shuts out virtually no one and welcomes diversity in all its facets, even religious; it celebrates the worth and dignity of all people; it defines itself through "deeds not creeds". So the soil is fertile; we just need to plant the right seeds and let them grow.

We cannot afford to be our own worst enemy. The dispossessed have enemies aplenty. We need to be at our best. We need to lead.

Most importantly, we need to cheer one another along in the inspiring process of healing our world. It is the essence of what makes us human. It is how we grow our soul.

ACKNOWLEDGEMENTS

It is impossible to acknowledge all the wonderful people who have helped make this book a reality. However, I would like to give a special thanks to four people who gave this manuscript a thorough edit and helped bring it to term, our Minister, Rev. Vanessa Rush Southern, our Board President, Tom Howard, Esq., my colleague on the Social Action Committee, Marty Rothfelder, Esq. and my partner, Roberta Renard. Without their painstaking effort to support this project, it would not have come to fruition.

I also wish to acknowledge the extraordinary work of the Unitarian Universalist Service Committee, which inspired me to undertake this project. In particular, I want to thank Rev. Dr. William F. Schulz, Charles Huschle and Lauralyn Smith for being of such enormous help in both seeing this through and offering unceasing encouragement.

I also want to acknowledge the wonderful members of our Social Action Committee at The Unitarian Church in Summit, whose drive and enthusiasm to heal our world is a daily inspiration.

Finally, I want to thank the congregation of The Unitarian Church in Summit as a whole. It is populated by an extraordinary group of people, all of whom have been incredibly supportive of our Committee's social action efforts. They continue to make this institution a welcoming place of happiness and good fellowship for all who enter its doors. I am honored to call them my friends.

About the Author

Gary D. Nissenbaum has been the Chair of the Social Action Committee of The Unitarian Church in Summit since 2005. In 2010, the congregation received the Unitarian Universalist Service Committee's Social Action Award. It was the first year such an award was given. That same year, it was also one of only two large congregations to receive the Unitarian Universalist Association's Breakthrough Congregation Award.

Mr. Nissenbaum is also a member of the Board of Trustees of the American Civil Liberties Union of New Jersey and serves as a cooperating attorney for that organization. He has published numerous articles on civil liberties issues for New Jersey Lawyer Magazine and is a frequent speaker on that topic to community groups, youth organizations and colleges.

Mr. Nissenbaum is the managing principal of the Nissenbaum Law Group, a commercial law firm with offices in New Jersey, New York, Texas and Pennsylvania. He is a former Chairman of the District XII Attorney Ethics Committee (Union County) and a current member of the New Jersey, New York, Texas and District of Columbia Bars. He is also a published novelist and a Tai Chi Chuan instructor.

Mr. Nissenbaum can be reached by email at gdn@gdnlaw.com.

CPSIA information can be obtained at www.ICGtesting.com
Printed in the USA
LVOW121812211211

260542LV00001B/41/P